D1519045

STATE LEGISLATIVE COMMITTEES
A STUDY IN PROCEDURE

SERIES XLIX   No 2

JOHNS HOPKINS UNIVERSITY STUDIES

IN

HISTORICAL AND POLITICAL SCIENCE

Under the Direction of the

Departments of History, Political Economy, and
Political Science

STATE LEGISLATIVE COMMITTEES

A STUDY IN PROCEDURE

BY

C. I. WINSLOW

GREENWOOD PRESS, PUBLISHERS
WESTPORT, CONNECTICUT

Library of Congress Cataloging in Publication Data

Winslow, Clinton Ivan.
   State legislative committees, a study in procedure.

   Reprint of the 1931 ed. published by the Johns Hopkins Press, Baltimore, as ser. 49, no. 2 of Johns Hopkins University studies in historical and political
science.
   Bibliography: p.
   1. Legislative bodies--Committees. 2. Legislative
bodies--United States--States. 3. Legislative bodies--
Maryland. 4. Legislative bodies--Pennsylvania.
I. Title. II. Series: Johns Hopkins University.
Studies in historical and political science, ser. 49,
no. 2.

JK2495.W5 1974   328.73'07'65   74-2797
ISBN 0-8371-7435-X

COPYRIGHT 1931 BY

THE JOHNS HOPKINS PRESS

Originally published in 1931 by The Johns Hopkins Press,
Baltimore

Reprinted in 1974 by Greenwood Press,
a division of Williamhouse-Regency Inc.

Library of Congress Catalog Card Number 74-2797

ISBN 0-8371-7435-X

Printed in the United States of America

PH 1-4-80

To O. E. W.

PIONEER, CITIZEN,

POLITICAL PRECEPTOR,

WITH FILIAL REGARD.

PREFACE

Standing committees in American legislative bodies have received considerable attention. Such writers as Woodrow Wilson, James Bryce, Robert Luce and L. G. McConachie have given especial consideration to the committees of the Congress of the United States. General treatments of state legislative committees are to be found, particularly in H. W. Dodd's *Procedure in State Legislatures* and in Robert Luce's *Legislative Procedure*. Treatises on state government, also, as a usual thing, pay a considerable amount of attention to committees. Detailed studies of committee systems in individual states are, however, comparatively rare. Dr. Horack's study of Iowa committees included in *Statute Law-Making in Iowa,* is the most complete one. For most of the states, no studies have been made.

It has been generally assumed that the committees in our state legislatures play an important role in legislation. The present study reveals that, in Maryland and Pennsylvania, during the sessions studied, committee action was really the final action in somewhat more than 92 per cent. of instances in the former state, and 83 per cent. in the latter. More detailed information in Chapter V shows how very important committees are in these two states. It is this very importance that justifies an investigation of committee systems.

Although intensive study was confined to systems in the two states mentioned above, it seemed desirable to look first at a wider field. Chapter I therefore offers, first, a brief summary of the rules of order in the forty-eight states in so far as they relate to the committees. The author contented himself with the rules as such, making no attempt to evaluate them or to describe legislative practice either aside from or contrary to the rules. The second part of the chapter presents certain statistical information as to the committee situation in the various states with a certain amount of interpretation. No claim is made that the quantitative measurements here or elsewhere in the study represent anything more than general tendencies.

The remaining chapters are devoted to an examination of the systems of standing committees in recent sessions of the Maryland and Pennsylvania legislatures. That there are other factors than those considered which affect the functioning of committees, is, of course, obvious. The personnel of the legislative bodies and the influence of representatives of interest-groups are among the most important of such factors. But they lie outside the scope of the present study.

Acknowledgements are due to a large number of persons whose names must be here omitted. But the author desires especially to express his appreciation to Professor Rodney L. Mott of the University of Chicago for originally suggesting the idea; to Dr. Horace E. Flack and his associates in the Maryland Department of Legislative Reference; to Miss Irma A. Watts and Mr. John H. Fertig of the Pennsylvania Legislative Reference Bureau; to members of the Department of Government in Harvard University; to his own associates in the Department of Political Science at Goucher College; and to numerous legislators and administrative officers in both Maryland and Pennsylvania, whose interviews and correspondence imparted much valuable information.

C. I. W.

CONTENTS

STATE LEGISLATIVE COMMITTEES
A STUDY IN PROCEDURE

CHAPTER I

RULES AND COMPOSITION OF STATE LEGISLATIVE COMMITTEES

A. Rules Governing Committees

A superficial survey of the committee systems in the ninety-six legislative bodies of our forty-eight states reveals remarkable similarities. So far as the published Rules of Order [1] reflect the actual situation, one is impressed that the differences should be so slight, considering the varying conditions under which they have developed. It would seem that here again, as is true so often in the history of American institutions, cultural and racial inheritances have counted for much more than environment. But, with all their surface similarities, the legislative committee systems have developed a sufficient number of original characteristics to make a review of them seem worth while.

1. Selection of Committee Members.

The importance of committees in the legislative process being recognized,[2] the method of assigning members to committees is of significance. In this, greater variation exists in state senates than in the lower houses. This would seem to be largely due to the existence in each of thirty-five states of a lieutenant-governor serving as presiding officer of the senate. In the thirteen state senates [3] electing their own chairman,

---

[1] The author was unable to find any complete collection of such rules. It required the cooperation of legislative reference libraries, secretaries of state, lieutenant-governors, speakers, clerks, college presidents, party committeemen, relatives and friends to complete the task.

[2] Certain statistical proof is adduced in ch. v.

[3] Arizona, Florida, Georgia, Maine, Maryland, Massachusetts, New Hampshire, New Jersey, Oregon, Tennessee, Utah, West Virginia, Wyoming. In Maine the Senate must consent to the appointments.

the appointing power rests without exception in his hands. This is similar to the general situation in the lower houses. But in the other thirty-five senates the location of the appointing power has been somewhat disturbed. In six cases,[4] the president *pro tempore,* elected from the senate membership, selects the committees. In eleven others,[5] the committees are elected by the senate, Nebraska providing for a special nominating committee to prepare the slate. In Montana, an elected committee of three members serves in an appointing capacity. A similar committee of five, the President and four elective members, acts in North Dakota. In Vermont, the appointing committee consists of the President, the President *pro tempore* and an elected member. The lieutenant-governors in the remaining fifteen states, with certain limitations, make the assignments.

These limitations, as set forth in the rules, are of three kinds. In the first place, the rules in Idaho, Mississippi and Washington require the consent of the senate to the committee selections. Secondly, specified committees in some states are excepted from the general rule. In Mississippi, the Committee on Rules consists of the Lieutenant-Governor, the President *pro tempore* and one senator from each of the congressional districts in the state elected by the senators from that district. The same committee in the Washington Senate consists of the president together with five senators from the western and four from the eastern part of the state. In Wisconsin, the Rules committee is composed, according to the rules, of the President *pro tempore* as chairman, the chairman of the joint committee on Finance, and that of each standing and special committee. In Virginia, it consists of the President, the President *pro tempore* and the chairman of the committee on Courts of Justice. And lastly, in senates having various forms of appointment, the number and size of the standing committees are usually provided in the rules.

[4] Connecticut, Delaware, Kentucky, Missouri, New York, Pennsylvania.

[5] Colorado, Illinois, Minnesota, Nebraska, New Mexico, Ohio, Oklahoma, Rhode Island, South Carolina, Virginia, Wisconsin. Minnesota adopted this practice in 1931.

The number seems to be set in all but Iowa. The size of each committee is definitely fixed in all save Delaware, Georgia, Illinois, Iowa, Kansas, Kentucky, Tennessee, Texas, Virginia, Indiana, North Carolina, South Carolina and West Virginia. In the last five of these, certain restrictions as to size are made. A maximum and minimum are set in South Carolina. The size of some and a maximum for others are provided in Indiana. A similar provision with a minimum added exists in West Virginia and Virginia, while North Carolina has an elastic maximum.[6] Beyond these, there are, of course, many restrictions—political and otherwise—not found in the rules, which set limits to the appointing power in the senates.

Turning to the lower houses, we find the statement of the situation much simpler. In all the states save Nebraska and Oklahoma, the rules place the appointing power solely in the speaker's hands.[7] The Nebraska method is set forth in Rule 21 as follows:

As near the commencement of the session as may be, the house shall elect a committee on committees composed of thirteen members, consisting of two members from each congressional district and one member at large who shall be chairman of the committee. This committee on committees shall as soon thereafter as possible recommend to the house for its approval and adoption the following standing committees, each with the number of members as hereinafter set out, and designating one member of each committee as chairman thereof.[8]

Rule 4 of the Oklahoma House provides:

Section 1. A committee of five members, consisting of three members belonging to the majority party in the House, and two members belonging to the minority party in the House, shall be elected by the members of the House, and shall be designated " Committee on Committees," and said committee shall select one of its members as Chairman, and shall appoint, subject to confirmation by the House, all standing committees of the House, with the right in its discretion to take from or add to said committees, subject to the confirmation by the House.[9]

---

[6] The rule provides a maximum of nine " unless the Lieutenant-Governor shall, without objection from the Senate, appoint a greater number on any committee." Rule 19, Senate Rules, 1929.

[7] The house rules in North Dakota, South Dakota and Wyoming do not specifically provide for appointment by the Speaker. Inquiry, however, confirms the inference that such is the case in the first two. The general nature of Wyoming's rules indicates a similar practice.

[8] Nebraska Legislative Manual, 1929, pp. 50-51.

[9] Rules of the House of Representatives, 1929, p. 9.

To be sure, the speaker's power of appointment is neither equal nor complete in the other forty-six states. Disregarding the limitations placed upon him by the party system, by unwritten rules or customs such as that of seniority, by the necessity of geographical distribution of appointments, highly important yet largely intangible restrictions, we find that the rules often provide boundaries to the speaker's sphere of power. Thus, in thirty-four states, including Nebraska, the rules, either of the house alone or the joint rules, provide the number and size of committees to be chosen. In thirteen other states, including Oklahoma, the number but not the size of committees is specified. In Iowa alone the rules contain no provision on either point. Among the thirteen states just mentioned, Kentucky, New Mexico, North Carolina and Tennessee say nothing as to size of committees. Georgia [10] and Montana provide maximum limits. Florida, Virginia [11] and West Virginia fix both minimum and maximum limits. Oregon specifies five members to each committee but permits the Speaker to increase one-third of the committees to seven, and one-third to nine members. Indiana sets an exact figure for five of the committees and a minimum and maximum figure for the remainder. The Committee on Committees in the Oklahoma house may fix and change the size of committees, subject to confirmation by the house. Pennsylvania alone establishes a minimum—and what a minimum it is! [12]

A second type of limitation is that of special provisions for special committees. The Maryland House Rules set geographical requirements for one committee, and fix the minority party representation upon all save that of Rules. In South Carolina, the Committee on Privileges and Elections must have one member from each congressional district. The Ways and Means committee in Kansas may not include a repre-

---

[10] Save in fifteen cases! Others have a maximum of twenty-five. Rule 197, Legislative Manual, 1927-28.

[11] The rules fix limits for certain separate committees and the exact sizes for some others. Rules 16, 17, 18 and 19, 1928.

[12] Rule 28 fixes a minimum of forty for one committee, of thirty-five for six others and of twenty-five for the remaining ones except that on Rules, which has five.

sentative from any district in which a state institution is
located. Certain membership on the Rules committee is
rather often specified.[13] But it can readily be seen that such
restrictions as the above must have but slight effect upon the
speaker's choice.

2. Reference of Measures.

Whether a bill be referred to one committee or to another
may obviously have considerable bearing upon its succeeding
history. A summary, therefore, of the rules intended to
control such reference will be of interest. The rules of the
upper houses in nine states have nothing at all to say on
this subject.[14] In eight others, the president is given the
power to refer, with no restrictions attached.[15] Thirteen
others specify the president as having power to refer; but
they place, or presume to place, certain restrictions upon him.
Arizona, Minnesota and Wyoming in this list specify merely
that reference must be to the "appropriate committee."
California, Indiana, Kansas, Montana, New Hampshire,
North Dakota and Wisconsin provide affirmatively that the
senate may refer or change the reference. New York requires
"consent of the Senate"; Oregon denies members of the senate
the right to have bills referred to committees where they do
not belong, and Vermont sets forth in detail the sphere of
each committee's work. Joint Rules in Maine provide a
Committee on Reference of Bills to suggest reference, and the
mover in the New Mexico Senate, subject to objection and
change by that body, indicates the proper reference on his
bill. In the other sixteen senates one finds such requirements
as "To the appropriate committee," "As a matter of course,"
"In regular order," but without any designation of authority.[16] It is to be presumed that the presiding officer exercises

---

[13] As in New York, where the Speaker is designated as chairman and
the majority leader as a member. Rule 2, secs. 8, 9.

[14] Arkansas, Florida, Georgia, Idaho, Mississippi, Nevada, Utah,
Washington, West Virginia.

[15] Illinois, Iowa, Kentucky, Maryland, Massachusetts, Michigan,
North Carolina, Pennsylvania.

[16] Louisiana provides that all bills and resolutions on the same
subject matter go to the same committee. Rule 40.

the power. But in some of these, as in some in the groups above, the scope of each committee's work is set forth in the rules.[17] Whether this controls the referring authority to any great extent may be doubted, but at any rate it indicates a desire to make the committees really specialized in their own fields.

Following the same order of consideration in the lower houses, we find no provisions respecting reference in eighteen states. The speaker, unhindered, is granted power in nine.[18] Certain restrictions are placed upon the speaker in ten others: the bill must go to the "appropriate" committee in Arizona, Maryland, Minnesota, North Carolina and New Hampshire, in the last of which, as in Nevada and Texas, the scope of each committee's work is put into the rules; the house must "consent" in New York; the house, by a two-thirds vote, may change the speaker's reference in Montana and, in Pennsylvania, a motion to refer is in order if the speaker fails to refer any measure within two days. Ohio provides a Reference Committee which, so far as the rules indicate, fixes the reference of bills. The joint committee in Maine, mentioned in connection with the senate, functions also for the house. The other seven states, without designating the authority, have such miscellaneous provisions as those already seen in senate rules: "To the appropriate committee," as in Colorado, North Dakota and West Virginia; "after first reading" in Alabama and Washington; and, in Connecticut and Missouri, statements of the scope of each committee's work. In many cases the rules require any measure affecting the state's finances to go finally to the finance committees. If we assume that silence in the rules leaves the power to refer in the hands of the speaker, this summary would indicate that he is practically unchecked in thirty-five states, checked only by indefinite phrases in six others and after a time limit in one, while in four the field for each committee is delimited and in two the reference is made by some other

[17] Connecticut, Missouri, Rhode Island, Vermont, Virginia.
[18] California, Idaho, Michigan, Mississippi, Nebraska, New Jersey, New Mexico, Utah, Virginia.

authority. To be sure, there doubtless exists in most states the possibility of changing the reference by action of the house. But a speaker, elected by a majority vote, is not likely to be overruled on such a point.

3. Meetings and Hearings.

In the senate rules of more than half the states, twenty-seven, to be exact, one finds no provisions respecting meetings or hearings by the committees. In Arizona, Kansas, Louisiana, Ohio and Pennsylvania the committees are expressly subject to call of their chairmen with the following conditions: the members to be notified in Arizona, a twelve hours' notice or announcement from the floor to be given in Louisiana, a majority of members in Ohio and the second named member in Pennsylvania to have power to issue a call if the chairman fails to do so. The Mississippi, Tennessee and Vermont [19] senates require announcements in open session with bulletin board notices in the last two. Regular schedules are provided for in the rules of Nebraska, Wisconsin and Vermont. In the first two of these, notice of the bills to be considered must be posted. In California the president is empowered to propose a schedule. Open committee meetings are required in Virginia except upon a recorded vote of the committee. They are also required in West Virginia and Iowa save for executive sessions while voting. Joint meetings of senate and house committees are provided for in Utah. Committee quorums are specified in some senate rules, a majority being designated in Arizona, Oregon, Utah, Virginia and Wisconsin, while Arkansas leaves the committee free to fix its own quorum.

With respect to committee hearings, the Joint Rules of the Massachusetts' General Court provide the necessity of notice to interested parties. A hearing is required in the Vermont Senate if requested, notice thereof being given. Committees in the upper houses of California, Indiana, Missouri, Ohio and Utah, must notify the author of the bill either before reporting adversely or before taking action. The author or

---

[19] Applies only to special meetings in Vermont.

2

any member of the House of Representatives may be heard upon request before any committee in the Oklahoma Senate. The joint rules in Vermont and Washington provide a means of holding joint hearings where the committees concerned so desire. Joint rules in Wisconsin require committee hearings to be open to the public.

The rules with respect to meetings and hearings are more numerous and varied in the lower houses. Here, in only fifteen cases are the rules entirely silent, although in Delaware the only rule is that committees may not sit during a session of the House without the Speaker's permission. Meetings are specifically subject to call by the chairman in Kansas, Texas, Vermont, Virginia and West Virginia, and impliedly so in Alabama and Illinois. Alabama provides for a call by the vice-chairman or next member if the chairman is absent, Illinois by fifty per cent. of the committee upon failure of the chairman. Kansas also provides for a call by the vice-chairman or upon the written request of three members. In six houses [20] announcement of committee meetings in open session is required while six [21] others require some sort of notice. Special committee meetings require one day's notice in Minnesota. The same provision, or a call by a majority of the committee, applies in New York. "Due notice" is necessary in Ohio and a posted notice is specified in Rhode Island and Washington. The Virginia house rules provide for notice to be given of the final voting time on measures under consideration. Other provisions respecting notice of meetings are found in Indiana where the notice must include the number of each bill to be considered; and in Texas where the notice must be posted as well as announced.

The practice of holding regular meetings is followed in some states. A schedule is required in California, Minnesota, Nebraska and Oregon. Regular meetings are to be provided for according to the rules in New York and Virginia and weekly meetings in New Jersey and Rhode Island, while

[20] Florida, Idaho, Indiana, North Dakota, Tennessee, Texas.
[21] Minnesota, New York, Ohio, Rhode Island, Virginia, Washington.

daily meetings are the order in Florida if any business exists. In Vermont the Speaker and the chairmen of committees may arrange stated meetings. Quorums are defined as consisting of a majority in Alabama, Illinois, Kentucky, Minnesota, New Jersey, New York, South Carolina, Texas and Washington. The committees may determine their own quorums in California and Mississippi but with a majority minimum in the former. It takes seven members or a majority in Iowa, the chairman and five members in North Carolina, and a majority or five members in the Virginia house committees, in order to do business. No rules are found in the other states regarding committee quorums, but it is presumed that a majority is necessary should a question arise.

Rules governing the matter of hearings before committees are found in only eight lower houses. New Hampshire requires a hearing, with one day's notice in the Journal, upon every bill referred to committees. Hearings are to be held in Vermont if requested. The mover or introducer is to be given a hearing in Illinois and Iowa. A hearing is granted by the chairman or by a majority of the committee to any interested person at any meeting of Colorado house committees. In Florida, notice is to be given to opponents and proponents of a measure. Hearings are to be announced and posted in New Jersey and one day's notice of public hearings is required in New York. As noted above,[22] the Joint Rules in Massachusetts, Vermont and Washington contain some provisions for joint hearings. Further miscellaneous rules require open meetings in Florida and Ohio, open hearings in Illinois, and in Iowa that the committee take no vote on the day of a public hearing.

4. Committee Records.

Requirements as to the keeping of records of committee proceedings are infrequent in both houses. In fifteen states only, do the rules have any provisions on this point, senate

---

[22] See pp. 17-18.

committees being affected in nine cases and house committees
in ten. Complete and detailed records of committee proceedings in both houses are required by the joint rules in
Wisconsin.[23] Joint rules in Iowa require records of the
Claims committee only. A record of the final vote of the
senate committee members on each bill is required to be kept
in Nebraska and New Jersey, while in California each committee report must show the number of committee members
favoring the report. Ohio's senate requires " a record of the
action " of the committee to be filed with the clerk of the
senate at the close of the session. The chairman of each
senate committee in West Virginia must have a record kept
of the time and place of each meeting and hearing showing
the attendance of members and the name of any person
appearing before the committee and the interest represented
by him. The clerk of the senate is to preserve this record.
It should be noted that the vote of the members is not a
requisite part of this record. The record in Vermont must
show the attendance of members at committee hearings, and
with respect to each bill the names of persons asking to be

---

[23] " Joint Rule 6. Record of committee proceedings.
1. The chairman or acting chairman of each committee of the
legislature shall keep, or cause to be kept, a record, in which
there shall be entered:
   (a) The time and place of each hearing, and of each meeting
       of the committee.
   (b) The attentance of committee members at each meeting.
   (c) The name of each person appearing before the commit-
       tee, with the name of the person, persons, firm or cor-
       poration in whose behalf such appearance is made.
   (d) The vote of each member on all motions, bills, resolu-
       tions and amendments acted upon.
2. Such record shall be ready and approved before the expiration
   of ten days after each committee meeting, or at the next regular meeting of the committee.
3. Every committee hearing shall be open to the public.
4. There shall be filed, in the proper envelope, with every bill or
   resolution reported upon, a sheet containing the foregoing information as to such bill or resolution, with a duplicate thereof
   to be filed by the chief clerk numerically by the number of the
   bill in such form to be most accessible for the use of the members and the public, during the session and at the end thereof
   in the office of the secretary of state."
The Assembly Manual, 1927, p. 279.

heard, the notice if any given them, and the dates of consideration of each bill with the vote of each member thereon. This record is to be public and, at the end of the session, to be filed with the Secretary of State. If any member of a committee or the author of the bill in the Minnesota senate should request it, a record of the votes on the report and on amendments must be made a part of the report.

The Vermont house rule is very similar to the senate rule given above. The joint rules in Iowa and Wisconsin apply, of course, also in the lower houses. Further, in the Iowa house, a record of the yeas and nays of committee members on the final vote on each measure is to be kept, except in the Appropriations and Judiciary committees. On demand of two members, the roll is called and a record kept in Nebraska house committees. Without such demand, only the vote of the committee appears in the report. In Florida the yea and nay vote must always be made a part of the committee's report. Each Ohio house committee must keep " a record of its proceedings, including the names of all persons who may appear before said committee." [24] The chairman of each committee in the Mississippi house must submit with his report a record of the time of meeting and adjournment of the committee with a list of the absent members. In Pennsylvania, a record of all proceedings must be kept, to be open for examination to members of the legislature and by leave of the committee to any one. The report of New York house committees must show the members present when the report was agreed to and how each member voted. The house rules in Illinois and Minnesota contain detailed provisions with respect to committee records, those in Illinois being almost identical with and obviously copied from the Wisconsin rule given earlier in this section. The Minnesota requirement is also the same except that the roll call, instead of being automatic, occures only upon demand of a committee member. No other rules are found in any state respecting committee records.

---

[24] Rule 64, Rules of the House of Representatives, 1929-30.

5. Committee Reports.

That ancient and revered (?) practice of " pigeon-holing " or " pickling " has been the cause of numerous and varied rules intended to keep the committee under the control of its parent body. In twenty-two senates the rules affirmatively state that committees shall report all measures, although definite enforcement provisions are not always existent. House rules in twenty-six cases, chiefly in the same states, provide similar requirements. Time limits for reports are set in twenty-three senates and in twenty-five lower branches. These are highly variable, ranging from three days in the Colorado Senate to twenty-five in that of Minnesota. The fiftieth day of the session seems to be the final dead-line in the Utah House and the Rhode Island Senate, while the thirty-fifth day requires immediate report in the Idaho House and for appropriation bills in the North Dakota Senate. The most frequent requirements are either ten or fifteen days. In a few states, outside the number mentioned above, the rules provide that reports must be made in a " reasonable " time, " as soon as practicable," " promptly," or " without unnecessary delay." Curiously enough, some rules, after providing a time limit, make no provisions for discharging a committee from consideration of a bill, while others fix a time after which a bill may be recalled without first affirmatively requiring the committee to report.

The method by which a legislative body recalls or may recall a measure from committee is an interesting and important part of committee procedure. The rules of order of eighteen senates and twenty-three houses seem to contain no provision whatever for such action. In the remaining states, the machinery of control varies all the way from the necessity of an extraordinary majority, with perhaps other special provisions, to a condition of automatic return. Taking up these various rules of control in order of their difficulty of application we have first, those requiring an extraordinary vote. A majority of the senators elected must support the recall measure in Delaware, Illinois, Kentucky, Mississippi (except in the last six days), Missouri, New York, Ohio and Rhode Island. The request must be written in Delaware. Two days' notice must be given in New York and one day in Illinois and Rhode Island, unless, in the last named state, a two-thirds vote is secured. In the lower houses a majority of the members elected is necessary in California, Illinois, Michigan, New Mexico, New York and Pennsylvania. A one-day notice is required in the Michigan House.

A second group of states permits the discharge of committees by a majority vote, sometimes with restrictions. Such are the rules in the upper houses of Arizona, California, Florida, Indiana (at any time), Minnesota, Mississippi (in the last six days), North Dakota (at any time), Oregon, Rhode Island (one day's notice), Tennessee, Virginia (two-thirds of the senators being present), Washington, Wisconsin and Wyoming (upon motion, seconded by three senators). Similar provisions exist in the lower houses of nine states: Alabama (one day's notice), Delaware (on petition), Georgia (one day's notice), Kentucky, Minnesota (at any time), North Carolina, Tennessee, Virginia (two-thirds being present) and Washington (after fifty days).

Special provisions, apparently easier of application than any of the above, occur in the rules of seven senates and five houses. In the senate of Colorado after three days, of Idaho after five, and of Indiana after six, any senator may upon one day's notice request the return of a bill from committee. Unless the senate thereupon extends the time for committee action, the bill must come back to the senate within three days in the first two cases and at once in the last. After twenty-five days, any Iowa senator who is the author of the bill in question may, upon request, have his measure returned immediately for consideration. A written petition of three senators in Maryland, of seven in New Jersey, and of five in South Dakota is sufficient to recall a bill, provided in the first of these that forty-five days have elapsed in case of the budget bill, twenty days for those referred in the first thirty days of the session and fifteen for those referred thereafter. No time limit appears in New Jersey and North Dakota. In these two and in Iowa there seems to be no provision permitting an extension of time by the senate.

The five house rules are so varied as to necessitate separate statement. After six legislative days have elapsed in the Florida House, any member favoring a measure may have it placed on the calendar. Idaho has a similar provision except that the time limit is decreased to five days with the possibility of an extension by the house. The Maryland House rule has the same time limits as that of the Senate, but no extension of time is provided for and the petition must be signed by fifteen members, a number slightly smaller in proportion to house size than that required in the Senate. In the Minnesota House, save for appropriation and claims bills, the author, after fifteen days, may request the return of his bill. If the committee then fails to report within seven days, the author has a five-day period in which to place the bill on general file. The New Jersey House rule provides simply that a petition of fifteen members requires a report within twenty-four hours.

There remains still that small group of states in which the bills upon certain conditions automatically come back to the houses for action. Bills must return from joint committees to the Massachusetts houses by the second Wednesday of March, if referred before March first, and in ten days if referred later. An extension of time is possible through a concurrent vote, but, without the recommendation of the Rules committee, such extension requires a four-fifths vote if it goes beyond the second Wednesday of April. The house rules, similarly, provide March tenth as a limit for bills referred to house committees before the first of March and allow two weeks for those referred later. In North Dakota, bills automatically return to the Senate after seven days, and to the House after ten days unless an extension of time is given. After fifteen days, all overdue bills in both Vermont houses are to be printed in the calendar. An immediate report is necessary after six days in the Texas House unless, by a two-thirds vote, added time is permitted. The Utah House rule puts all bills automatically on the calendar after fifteen days in committee, an extension of time being permitted by action of the House. All reports, moreover, are to be in before the fiftieth day of the session. In the states not enumerated in the above paragraphs no affirmative provision for discharging a committee from consideration of a measure is found. In the case of the Pennsylvania Senate a rule provides that no committee shall be so discharged within five days except by unanimous consent. Presumably, in the remaining legislatures, bills may be recalled by action of the chamber, a majority vote, or at most a majority of the entire membership, being sufficient.

While the subject of committee reports is under consideration, a few statements should be made concerning the privileged position occupied by some committees in some states in the matter of the time for reporting. Such committees as those on Engrossed Bills, Enrolled Bills, Revision of Bills, and Printing are frequently permitted to report at any time. Conference committees, which are not, of course, part of the standing system, are also often so privileged. The Committee on Rules in the senates of Georgia, Indiana, Iowa, Massachusetts, Mississippi, New Mexico, New York, Oklahoma and South Dakota is granted such a position in the standing rules. The sister committee in the lower branch is permitted to report at any time by the rules in Alabama, Arizona, Colorado, Maryland and Texas. Other privileged committees in the senates are those on Elections in Colorado, Indiana, Mississippi, New York and South Dakota; on Finance in Colorado and Mississippi; on Appropriations in Oklahoma; and the Executive committee in New Mexico. In the houses, the committee on Elections is privileged in Arizona, Colorado, Maryland and Montana; the Ways and Means committee in Arizona, Colorado, Indiana, Maryland and Montana; the Appropriations committee in Arizona, Colorado and Montana; and the committee on Constitutional Amendments and Referendum in Arizona. The Elections committee, of course, will be chiefly concerned with disputed seats and like questions, its privileged position in some states being limited to such cases. The significance of the position held by the

Rules committee lies in its ability to affect thereby the order of consideration of bills on the calendar. The primary position held by the committees dealing with state finance in most states is emphasized by giving them this added prestige.

6. Conference Committees.[25]

The rules in at least thirty-one state legislatures make some provision respecting committees of conference. In most part these are to be found in the joint rules, with occasional additions in the rules of the individual houses. At least one case, that of Missouri, exhibits a constitutional provision. These regulations, when thrown together, can be placed mostly under four chief headings: the composition of the committee, the scope of its work, the requirement as to agreeing upon a report, and, lastly, the conditions precedent to action by the houses upon the report.

Three members of each house compose the committee in California, Maine, Massachusetts, Ohio, Oklahoma, Utah, Vermont, Washington and Wisconsin. The members are to be chosen from those who voted in the majority according to Maine and Massachusetts provisions, while both majority and minority, if possible, are to be represented in California and Washington committees. Other provisions as to size of conference committees are as follows: Colorado, two senators and three representatives; Connecticut, one senator and two representatives; Iowa, four from each house; Maryland, not to exceed five from the senate (no House rule exists); Minnesota, from three to five from each; Montana and Nevada, equal numbers from each; New York, three senators and five delegates; Texas, five from each house. These are to be from the majority on the measure in question in Connecticut and Delaware, as is also true in Georgia, where the number is fixed by motion, and in Pennsylvania. In Iowa, the Executive Committee selects the senate members; in Maryland, the Senate acts by ballot.

---

[25] These are not, of course, standing committees but their importance in some systems seemed to warrant their inclusion.

As to the scope of the committee's work, the states are in two main groups. In one of these, the conference committees are limited in their report to the point or points of difference between the houses. This group includes Colorado (except for the last three days of the session), Delaware, Georgia, Illinois (on appropriation bills), Iowa, Kansas (by senate rule only), Nevada, New York, Ohio, Oklahoma, Pennsylvania, Texas,[26] Utah, Washington and Wisconsin. The states in which the rules seem to permit free conference, the points of difference not being the limits, are Illinois (except for appropriation bills), Montana, Nebraska, North Dakota, Vermont, and in Nevada and Washington after the first attempt at limited conference fails. One difficulty in attempting to restrict the committee may arise, of course, when the second house has so completely changed the original bill as to make the " points of difference " as wide as the measure itself. In addition, the practice in Texas, as indicated in the note, may come far from being an exception.

Only a few states have requirements on the method of committee agreement. But in California, four members must agree, while in Illinois, Iowa, Maine, Massachusetts, New York, Oklahoma and Texas a majority of the representatives from each house must agree to the report.

Before the committee report can be acted upon, certain conditions must be met in a few states. The report must be printed in Colorado, and, in Nebraska, upon the request of five members. Otherwise, in the last named state, the report must be read and the numbers of all bills affected be displayed before the house for two hours unless unanimously accepted. Reading is required also in Indiana (with a one-day delay), New York, Utah and Washington.

Certain miscellaneous provisions complete the list of thirty-one states. The Idaho rules provide that, if the report is

---

[26] In practice, says a note in the manual, " ' Free ' Conference Committees are generally appointed " and " have often exercised plenary powers in that they have not confined their reports to the matter disagreed upon between the two houses, but have gone outside of that and in many instances have brought in entirely new bills." Legislative Manual, Forty-first Legislature, p. 227.

made up of more than one part, concurrence may be divisible.
The yeas and nays of a constitutional majority are required
by the Constitution of Missouri. In the Montana House of
Representatives, the report must carry a statement of the
effects of the agreement upon the measure. The New Jersey
and South Dakota rules go no farther than to provide that
conference committees may be appointed, while the South
Carolina joint rules make provision for a " Committee of
Free Conference " without any special requirements. Whatever restrictions rest upon such committees in these three
states, as indeed upon many of the others (including seventeen states not here enumerated), must be found outside the
published rules.

7. Steering Committees.

Although steering or sifting committees can hardly be
said to be part of the standing committee system, their
influence in determining the course of legislative procedure
is of sufficient importance to justify a survey of legislative
rules affecting them. In fifteen states such committees are
definitely provided for in the rules of one, or both houses.
In the Arizona Senate, for the last ten days of the session or
such other time as the Senate may determine, the Rules Committee, plus four senators appointed by the president, has
authority to present rules " designating the order in which bills
or measures shall be considered by the Senate or by the Committee of the Whole, which rules shall in all cases be deemed
standing rules of the Senate." [27] The Rules Committee of
the Georgia Senate, during the last fifteen legislative days of
each session arranges the calendar for each day, no change in
such program to be made save by a three-fourths vote.[28] The
Executive Committee in the Illinois Senate may report a
special order for the day, subject to suspension, amendment or
modification on roll-call by a majority of the senators
present.[29] The president of the Iowa Senate may propose a

[27] Rule X, section 10. Senate Rules, 1929.
[28] Rule 45, Legislative Manual, 1927-28.
[29] Rule 63, Handbook, Illinois Legislature, 1929.

sifting committee at any time subject to the consent of the
Senate, the appointment being made by the president.[30]   The
Kansas rule is for a committee of five members on Revision
of the Calendar, appointed by the president.   This committee
" shall designate from day to day and from time to time the
bills for consideration that day and the next legislative day,
and the order of the revision committee shall not be changed
except by a two-thirds vote of the Senate." [31]   The Rules
Committee of the Kentucky Senate becomes the steering committee for the last fifteen days of the session.[32]   The Massachusetts joint rules provide that " The committee on Rules,
together with the presiding officers of the two branches, acting
concurrently, may consider and suggest such measures as
shall, in their judgment, tend to facilitate the business of the
session." [33]   The Nebraska Senate may provide a sifting committee of seven members elected by the senate to have charge
of all bills on general file, arranging them, save for appropriation bills and claims, in order of their precedence before the
Senate.[34]   A steering committee of seven members may be
provided in the Ohio Senate by action of two-thirds of the
members elected, but it may not put on the calendar any
measure in the possession of a committee.[35]   The Committee
on Rules and Procedure of the Oklahoma Senate is to super-
vise and arrange the daily calendar.[36]   In Washington, the
Committee on Rules and Joint Rules has a similar duty, with
the provision that the Senate may by a majority vote advance
any bill to any place on the calendar.[37]

In addition to Massachusetts, whose joint rule cited above
provides for " steering " in the lower house, ten other states
have house steering committees officially provided for.   The
Rules committee acts in such capacity in all these except two

---

[30] Rule 40, Rules of Procedure, 1929.
[31] Rule 71, Rules for the Senate, 1929.
[32] Section 44, F. K. Kavanaugh, Kentucky Directory, 1928.
[33] Joint Rule 1, Manual for the General Court, 1929-30, p. 624.
[34] Rule 13, Nebraska Legislative Manual, 1929.
[35] Rule 115, Rules of the Senate, 1929.
[36] Rule 4, Rules of the Senate, 1929.
[37] Rule 8, 1929 Legislative Manual.

—Kansas and Nebraska. In Kansas the speaker appoints, on
or about the thirtieth day of the session, a committee on
revision of the calendar composed of five members.[38] The
Nebraska House, " whenever it shall appear advisable or
necessary," elects a sifting committee of thirteen members,
two chosen by and from the delegation from each congressional district in addition to the speaker who acts as chairman.[39] Time limits are set in Georgia, Kentucky and New
York. The rules committee acts as a steering agency in the
first of these only in the last fourteen days of the session,
fifteen in the second and ten in the last. In Georgia, a
majority vote of all members elected is necessary to change
the program fixed by the committee. Colorado, Idaho, Illinois, North Carolina and Washington complete the list of
states designating the Rules committee as a steering agency,
none of these having any special provisions.

In states having no special provisions for a steering committee it is presumed that the committee on Rules in senate
and house can introduce special rules to accomplish the end
of advancing measures on the calendar. This, of course,
may be suggested by an unofficial steering group, as is the
practice in the national House of Representatives.

The position occupied by the rules committee assumes added
significance when its composition is noted. The size is usually
rather small, three or five members being frequent. Relatively
large committees are found in a few upper houses: Georgia
has nineteen members, Kentucky seventeen, Illinois thirteen,
Mississippi, North Carolina, Washington and Wisconsin ten
each. Similarly in the lower houses, Georgia heads the list
for large rules committees with one of thirty-nine members.
Kentucky, North Carolina, Florida and Massachusetts have
sixteen, fourteen, thirteen and twelve members respectively.
Alabama, Missouri, New York and Rhode Island have eleven
each. It is, however, the smaller committees rather than the
larger that deserve attention as to membership. The end-of-
the-session rush, so familiar in American legislative bodies,

---

[38] Rule 16, Rules for the House, 1929.
[39] Rule 22, Nebraska Legislative Manual, 1929.

centralizes power in that group which controls the calendar. If that be the committee on rules and it be small, the control of legislation is highly concentrated. The membership of the Rules committees, then, is of especial significance.

The power to select committee members, which as a general thing includes the Rules committee with the rest, has been discussed above.[40] The actual membership, in so far as it has been possible to ascertain it for the regular sessions, is set forth below. In the senates it is found that the president is chairman of the Rules committee in nine states.[41] In two others,[42] he is a member only. The president *pro tempore* is chairman in ten states [43] and a member in eleven others.[44] Neither of the two is on the Rules committee in ten other senates [45] and the president is not found to be a member in seven.[46] No information on Rules committees is contained in the rules or lists of committees of the Maine, Pennsylvania or Rhode Island senates.

On the house side, the speaker more frequently occupies a position on the Rules committee and, as has been pointed out before, possesses greater appointive power generally than the senate's presiding officer. In twenty states [47] the speaker is chairman of the Rules committee. In six others [48] he is a member. The speaker *pro tempore* is found to be a member

---

[40] See pp. 11-15.

[41] Arizona, Georgia, Maryland, Massachusetts, West Virginia, Kentucky, Mississippi, Virginia, Washington. In the last four the Lieutenant-Governor is president.

[42] New Hampshire, South Dakota (Lieutenant-Governor).

[43] Alabama, California, Delaware, Iowa, Montana, New York, North Carolina, Ohio, Rhode Island, Wisconsin.

[44] Georgia, Illinois, Indiana, Kansas, Kentucky, Maryland, Mississippi, Oklahoma, Vermont, Virginia, Washington.

[45] Arkansas, Connecticut, Florida, Idaho, Louisiana, Michigan, Nevada, North Dakota, South Carolina, Texas.

[46] Colorado, Minnesota, Missouri, New Mexico, Oregon, Tennessee, Utah.

[47] Alabama, Arizona, Delaware, Georgia, Illinois, Indiana, Kentucky, Maine, Maryland, Massachusetts, Mississippi, New Hampshire, New Mexico, New York, Ohio, Vermont, Virginia, Washington, West Virginia, Wyoming.

[48] California, Colorado, Montana, Pennsylvania, South Dakota, Wisconsin.

in six cases only,[49] but information on this point is not generally available. The speaker is definitely found not to be a member in nineteen cases [50] and the speaker *pro tempore* in four.[51] No committee on rules is evident from the information available on the Nevada House of Representatives.

B. COMMITTEE STATISTICS

1. Joint Committee Systems.

The joint committee system, as is well known, predominates in Connecticut, Maine and Massachusetts. A summary of the number and size of such committees, together with those of the separate houses and the resulting average number of committee assignments for each legislator, is shown in the accompanying table.

TABLE 1. COMMITTEE COMPOSITION.[1]

| | Joint Committees | | | | | Separate Committees | | | | | | Assignments | | | |
| | | Size | | | | Senate | | | House | | | No. of Aver. Sen. Assign. | | No. of Aver. Rep. Assign. | |
	No.	Sen.	Rep.	Total	Aver.	No.	Size	Aver.	No.	Size	Aver.	No.	Aver.	No.	Aver.
Conn.²	37	2³	13⁴	15	14.3	2	3	3	1	3	3	35	2.3	262	1.7
Maine	38⁵	3	7	10	10-	2	12	12	7	3-16⁶	8-	31	4.5	151	2.1
Mass {	7	3	8	11 } 14-		5	3-7	5-	7	3-13	7.3	40	3.5-	240	1.5
{	23	4	11	15 }											

[1] All statistical data in tables in Chapter I are compiled from official lists, manuals, handbooks, etc., secured from the forty-eight states.

² Seven committees, chiefly honorary in character—four of the senate and three joint—are omitted.

³ One committee has three senators instead.

⁴ One committee has only two house members, another has three, and a third has eight.

⁵ One committee has only two senators and three house members.

⁶ Mostly of seven members; Rules has three; County Estimates, sixteen.

It will be readily seen that the joint committees occupy most of the field. There are, however, sufficient separate committees

---

[49] Florida, Montana, Rhode Island, Georgia, New York, Ohio. (Vice-Chairman in the first three).

[50] Arkansas, Connecticut, Florida, Idaho, Iowa, Kansas, Louisiana, Michigan, Maine, Missouri, New Jersey, North Carolina, North Dakota, Oregon, Rhode Island, Tennessee, Texas, Utah, South Carolina.

[51] Kansas, Maryland, Missouri, South Carolina.

to justify attention. In Connecticut the only Senate committees are on Senate Appointments and Executive Nominations; in the House, only on Elections. A Rules committee of three members is listed in the 1929 *Manual* but no rule provides for it. All four of these, obviously, are concerned with matters peculiar to their respective houses. The Senate committees in Maine are on Bills in Second Reading and on Engrossed Bills, not concerned, of course, with the subject matter of legislation. In the House, however, in addition to committees on Bills in the Third Reading and on Engrossed Bills, there are provided one on Leave of Absence, one on Elections and one on Rules and Business of the House. All of these are procedural in nature rather than substantive. A committee on Ways and Means and one on County Estimates completes the list. Each house of the Massachusetts General Court has committees on Bills in Third Reading, Engrossed Bills, Rules, Judiciary, and Ways and Means with definite provision for joint meetings of the last two if the chairmen so decide, or by reference. Other than the above the House has a committee on Elections and one on Pay Roll. From this enumeration it is evident that separate committees occupy a comparatively small place in the committee system of these three states, save for the normally important position of financial and judicial committees.[52]

Joint committees of various sorts are provided for in the rules of eighteen other state legislatures and, in at least one case, in the constitution. In California, Washington, Utah and Wisconsin, the rules make possible joint meetings or hearings on the part of similar committees in the two houses, usually at the discretion of the chairmen. This practice hardly justifies inclusion in this section and is followed in some states where no such provision exists in the rules. Joint investigatory committees are provided for in Arkansas, Mississippi and New Jersey. They are limited to the Treasurer's

---

[52] For a description and evaluation of joint committees in Massachusetts, see A. C. Hanford, " Our Legislative Mills: Massachusetts Different from the Others," in National Municipal Review, 13: 40-48 (1924).

3

Books in the last, extend to the Auditor, the Commissioner of
State Lands and the Superintendent of Public Instruction in
the first, and to all state offices in Mississippi.   The Constitu-
tion of Maryland requires a similar joint committee.   Certain
formal committees are provided in eleven states: California
has a committee on Revision and Printing; Illinois, one to
examine bills after passage; Indiana, Iowa, Mississippi, New
Hampshire and West Virginia each one on Enrolled or
Engrossed Bills; New Jersey, Rhode Island, Virginia and
Wyoming, each one on Printing; New Jersey, another on
Passed Bills; and Rhode Island, another on Law Revision.
Joint committees on Rules are provided in California,
Indiana, New Hampshire,[53] North Dakota, Rhode Island and
Vermont.

In addition to the investigatory, formal and procedural
committees listed above, there are two other main groups of
joint committees.   The largest of these in point of number of
committees may possibly be labelled supervisory.   They have
to do with state institutions or property such as the state
library, the state-house, charitable institutions, and so forth.
Indiana and Virginia have one such committee each,
Arkansas, Mississippi and New Hampshire each two, North
Dakota has five, and New Jersey fifteen.   The other group
includes those of a financial nature.   Thus, Arkansas has a
Budget committee, Mississippi has one on the Executive Con-
tingent Fund, New Jersey one on Sinking Fund, Rhode Island
one on Accounts and Claims, Virginia one on Auditing,
and Wisconsin has one on Finance required by statute.

Besides the above five groups, four states have certain
miscellaneous joint committees.   North Dakota has one
committee on Insurance and one on Labor; Rhode Island has
one each on Sales of Real Estate (perhaps belonging in the
fourth group above), Executive Communications and Public
Health; Vermont has three Canvassing committees; and
Virginia has one each on Confirmation and on Special,
Private and Local Legislation.   Other than as indicated by the

[53] This joint committee seems to be in existence although no provision is found in the rules.

existence of the above joint committees the committee systems of forty-five state legislatures are organized on a bicameral basis. To these we now direct attention.

2. Bicameral Committee Systems.

A summary view of statistical information on legislative committees is given in Table 2. The columns headed " Number" do not include joint committees. Neither do those listing the average committee sizes. The latter columns show merely, for the senates and the lower houses, the arithmetical mean of all one-house committees in each state. As note (3) of the table indicates, assignments to joint committees are included in computing the average committee assignments of members.

A casual view discloses some rather startling facts. The very large number of committees, the large average size, and the large number of assignments to each member in many states are, perhaps, the first items to attract attention. Eight senates have more than forty committees each while only four have less than twenty.[54] This fact of numerous committees is particularly significant when it is noted that the average number of members in the senate is 37.5. On the house side, ten states show more than fifty committees each and sixteen show more than forty each. At the bottom end of the scale only one house has less than twenty committees and eleven have less than thirty. With the larger house membership— an average of 114—the existence of so many committees is not apt to be so burdensome to the members unless the size of the committees is proportionally larger than in the upper houses. This in general is not the case.

How can the prevalent large number of committees be explained? In the first place, there are usually some committees—from a few to many—of a non-substantive nature. Such are the rules committees in both houses found nearly everywhere. Such formal committees as those on Printing,

---

[54] Table 3, pp. 40-41, shows the arrangement of states in order of number of members, number of committees, and average committee size.

Enrolled or Engrossed Bills, Bill Revision and Style, account for part of the number although in many cases the work of such committees is done rather by employees. Another class of committees is that of a supervisory nature with the supposed duty of visiting various state institutions or supervising the State Library or Capitol Building. Occasionally these are rather numerous. In Michigan twenty-seven of the

TABLE 2.   COMMITTEE COMPOSITION.[1]

	Senate Size						House Size					
	No.	Min. Max.	Most Fre.[2]	Aver.	No. of Sen.	Aver. Assign.[3]	No.	Min. Max.	Most Fre.[2]	Aver.	No. of Rep.	Aver. Assign.[3]
Ala.	28	3–15	5	7.6	35	6–	40	5–31		15.7	106	6–
Ariz.	22	3– 7	15	4.8	19	5.8	27	3–17	8	7.7	54	4–
Ark.	40	3–14	5	5.9	34	7–	41	3–21	7	9.0	100	3.
Cal.	40	3–17	5	8.7	40	8.8	58	3–21	7–9	10.4	80	7.
Colo.	29	4–17		8.0	35	6.7	37	5–13	9	9.5	65	5.
Del.	23	5– 5	5	5.0	17	6.8	27	3– 5	5	5.0	35	4.
Fla.	40	3–17	5	6.3	38	7–	69	5–17	9	10.3	95	7.
Ga.	48	4–27		12.6	51	12–	51	14–75		35.6	207	8.
Idaho	28	3–11		6.5	44	4.1	39	3–11	5–7	6.3	68	3.
Ill.	41	3–51		23.0	51	18.5	32	5–58		25.4	153	5.
Ind.	48	3–13	7	7.6	50	7.5	58	5–13	13	12.3	100	7.
Iowa	51	5–27		10–	50	10.0	48	5–54		17.8	108	7.
Kans.	43	5–11	5	6.8	40	7.4	37	5–24		11.6	125	3.
Ky.	39	6–16	7	7.4	38	7.6	66	9–19	9	9.1	100	6.
La.	26	5–15		9.5	39	6.4	37	6–21	9	10.8	100	4.
Md.	29	3–12	9	8.9	29	9.3	35	4–22	9	9.6	118	3.
Mich.	38	3–13	5	5.4	32	6.4	62	5–13	5	6.2	100	3.
Minn.	40	9–30	15	13.0	67	7.9	46	5–35		18.1	131	6.
Miss.	37	3–13	9	7.8	49	6.4	39	5–46		16.4	140	4.8
Mo.	24	5–13	7	8.0	34	5.6	55	6–46	11	13.7	150	5.0
Mont.	39	3– 9		6.1	56	4.3	51	3–17	15	11.4	100	0.
Neb.	31	3–11	7	7.8	33	7.0	30	3–11		8.2	100	2.5
Nev.	25	3– 5	3–5	4–	17	5.7	29	3– 7	5	4.7	37	3.7
N. H.	24	3– 5	5	5–	24	5.1	32	3–19	17	16.4	421	1.
N. J.	26	3– 4	3	3	19[4]	7.6	31	5– 5	5	5.0	60	4.2
N. M.	18	5– 9	7	7–	24	5.2	31	3–13		6.8	49	4.
N. Y.	27	5–16		8.0	51	4.2	33	7–15	13	12.9	150	2.8
N. C.	51	10–23		13–	50	13.2	53	7–28		15.6	120	6.9
N. D.	35	3–23	9–11	10.3	49	8.5	34	3–49	9–17	13.3	113	4.5
Ohio	21	5–14	7– 9	9–	31	6.0	36	4–23		13.0	133	3.5
Okla.	37	5–18		10.1	44	8.5	29	5–28		15.1	104	4.2
Ore.	35	3– 9	5	5.2	30	6.0	36	3– 9	5–7	6.2	60	3.8
Pa.	35	6–37		18.7	50	13.1	44	6–52	25	30.4	208	6.5
R. I.	11	5– 9		7–	39	2.5	14	9–11	11	10.2	100	1.8

TABLE 2.　COMMITTEE COMPOSITION (Continued).

	No.	Senate Size Min. Max.	Most Fre.[2]	Aver.	No. of Sen.	Aver. Assign.[3]	No.	House Size Min. Max.	Most Fre.[2]	Aver.	No. of Rep.	Aver. Assign.[3]
S. C.	29	6–18		11.5	46	7.3	25	3–35		13.4	124	2.7
S. D.	53	3–15	7	7.5	45	8.8	59	3–15	7	8.6	103	5.0
Tenn.	34	4–20		9.6	33	10–	44	9–29		20.5	99	9.2
Tex.	36	3–15		9.2	31	10.7	38	5–21	21	16.9	150	4.3
Utah	12	3– 9	5–7	5.8	20	3.7	30	3–13		6.4	55	3.5
Vt.	31	3–14	5	5.4	30	5.8	26	5–15	15	14.3	250	1.5
Va.	20	3–17	3–11	9.0	40	5–	26	3–21	13	13.5	100	3.8
Wash.	51	3–18	5– 7	7.3	42	9–	49	4–30	5	9.5	97	4.9
W. Va.	26	4–17	9	9.7	30	8.6	28	9–22	15	15.3	94	4.7
Wis.	9	3–10	5	5.1	33	1.5	22	3–11		7.0	100	1.6
Wyo.	25	2– 5	3–5	4.1	27	4–	29	5– 9	7	7.0	62	3.3
Average	32.3			8.6	37.5	7.6	39.2			12.8	114	4.5

[1] Statistics are for the 1929 sessions except as follows: Alabama, 1927; Kentucky, 1928; Louisiana, 1928; Mississippi, 1928; Virginia, 1928. Connecticut, Massachusetts and Maine are in Table 1.

[2] Where committees are chiefly of one or two sizes, it is so indicated.

[3] In computing figures in these two columns, assignments to joint committees have been included where they exist. Such committees have not been included in computing the average size of committees in the fourth and tenth columns.

[4] The Senate regularly has twenty-one members. Two vacancies in 1929 raised the committee assignments.

sixty-two house committees are of this type, if the committee names indicate their functions. Supervisory committees do, of course, on occasion receive bills for consideration but the total number of measures so referred must be slight. Investigatory committees are apt to be either joint or special and do not often affect the standing committee situation. The Oklahoma House has such a standing committee composed of thirty-two members. There are, however, certain miscellaneous committees in one or the other of the houses which should be noted. Committees to canvass election returns or look into the qualifications of members, committees for the employment or supervision of legislative employees, committees on incidental chamber expenses or claims,—these account for a certain number in nearly all legislative bodies. In the senates, a committee on Executive Nominations is widely prevalent. The exact percentage of the total number of committees to be classed in the above groups is not known, chiefly because the rules of the houses do not generally indicate the nature of the work of each committee and the name is not always a reliable guide. To a certain extent the above groups do participate in legislation but generally they receive few, if any, measures for consideration. They do, however, markedly swell the total number of committees and accordingly the committee assignments of members, whether they add materially to the duties of legislators or not.

A second explanation of the number of committees may lie in the size of the respective bodies. Whether the relationship between number of members and number of committees is causal would be difficult to say. However, there may be certain significance in the following comparison. Reference to Table 3 discloses that of the nine largest senates and the nine having the largest number of committees, five are the same. The next largest number of such coincidences occurs with size-group II, showing three correlations, while size-groups III, IV, and V contain only one case. At the bottom end, five of the nine smallest senates show five of the nine smallest number of committees, with size-groups IV, III, II, and I coinciding with the senates of smallest committee numbers in 2, 2, 0 and 0 times respectively. It may be noted that in three cases the number of senators and of committees is coincident, that in five there is a variation of only one, in four of only two and in three of only three. In other words, in one-third of the senates the number of committees is within three of the number of senators. Further, these close relationships exist throughout the list, there being four in size-group I, two in group II, two in group III, three in group IV, and four in group V.

In the lower houses, however, such relationships are less frequent. Houses in size-group I show only two cases of coincidence with the houses having the largest number of committees while one is among the houses with the smallest number. Of the other size-groups, two of number I, four of number III, one of number IV, and none of group V have committees numbering among the first nine. Among the houses having the smallest number of committees, three belong to size-group V, four to size-group IV, none to group III, one to group II and one to group I. Although not so marked as in the senates, a tendency is seen even here for the number of committees to be larger wherever the number of members is larger.

Is there a similar relationship between the number of members and the average size of committees? The answer would seem to be in the affirmative, the correlation being even greater. In the various size-groups of the senates we find group I has six among the nine having the largest average committees, group II has three and groups III, IV, and V have none. At the lower end of the scale, group V has six among the smallest average committees, group IV has three, and the three other larger size-groups have none. In the lower houses, group I has six among the nine having the largest average committees, group II has two and group IV has one, while groups III and V have none. At the bottom of the list group V has seven among those having the smallest average committees with groups IV and III having one each, and groups I and II having none. Such correlation between the size of the chamber and committee size could hardly be a mere coincidence.

Another and important factor affecting the number of committees is the existence or continuance of dead or useless organizations. It is not suggested that dead committees exist in all the states, but that they do in a great many is beyond question. Committees are created to serve some real or apparent need. They consider measures and flourish like a green bay tree, perhaps for a session, or a few sessions, or even many sessions. Each succeeding session adopts the rules of the preceding one, the list of committees included. Those committees that have outlived their usefulness are easier to retain than to abolish. Besides, they may serve some purpose other than that of considering proposed legislation. Certain emoluments of intrinsic worth or of indirect value often appertain to committee positions. There may be an office with secretarial help, or at least with secretarial allowance;

TABLE 3. MEMBERSHIP AND COMMITTEE COMPOSITION.

	SENATE					HOUSE			
No. of Sen.		No. of Com.		Size of Com.	No. of Rep.		No. of Com.		Size of Com.

Size-Group I.

No. of Sen.		No. of Com.		Size of Com.	No. of Rep.		No. of Com.		Size of Com.
67	Minn.	53	Ill.	23.0	421	Fla.	69	Ga.	35.6
56	Mont.	51	Pa.	18.7	250	Ky.	66	Pa.	30.4
51	Ga.	51	N. C.	13.0	208	Mich.	62	Ill.	25.4
51	Ill.	51	Minn.	13.0	207	S. D.	59	Tenn.	20.5
51	N. Y.	48	Ga.	12.6	153	Ind.	58	Minn.	18.1
50	Ind.	48	S. C.	11.5	150	Cal.	58	Ia.	17.8
50	Ia.	43	Ind.	10.3	150	Mo.	55	Tex.	16.9
50	N. C.	41	Okla.	10.1	150	N. C.	53	N. H.	16.4
50	Pa.	40	Ia.	10.0	140	Ga.	51	Miss.	16.4

Size-Group II.

No. of Sen.		No. of Com.		Size of Com.	No. of Rep.		No. of Com.		Size of Com.
49	Cal.	40	W. Va.	9.7	133	Ohio	51	Ala.	15.7
49	Fla.	40	Tenn.	9.6	131	Minn.	49	N. C.	15.6
46	Minn.	40	La.	9.5	125	Kan.	48	W. Va.	15.3
45	Ky.	39	Tex.	9.2	124	S. C.	46	Okla.	15.1
44	Mont.	39	Ohio	9.0	120	N. C.	44	Vt.	14.3
44	Mich.	38	Va.	9.0	118	Md.	44	Mo.	13.7
42	Miss.	37	Md.	8.9	113	N. D.	41	Va.	13.5
40	Okla.	37	Cal.	8.7	108	Iowa	40	S. C.	13.4
40	Tex.	36	Colo.	8.0	106	Ala.	39	N. D.	13.3

Size-Group III.

No. of Sen.		No. of Com.		Size of Com.	No. of Rep.		No. of Com.		Size of Com.
40	N. D.	35	Mo.	8.0	104	Miss.	39	Ohio	13.0
39	Ore.	35	N. Y.	8.0	103	Tex.	38	N. Y.	12.9
39	Pa.	35	Miss.	7.8	100	Kan.	37	Ind.	12.3
38	Tenn.	34	Neb.	7.8	100	Ind.	37	Kan.	11.6
38	Neb.	31	Ala.	7.6	100	La.	37	Mont.	11.4
35	Vt.	31	Ind.	7.6	100	Colo.	36	La.	10.8
35	Colo.	29	S. D.	7.5	100	Ohio	36	Ohio	10.4
34	Md.	29	Ky.	7.4	100	Ore.	36	Cal.	10.4
34	S. C.	29	Wash.	7.3	100	Md.	35	Fla.	10.3
					100	N. D.	34	R. I.	10.2

SENATE

Size-Group IV.

State	No. of Sen.	State	No. of Com.	State	Size of Com.
Neb.	33	Ala.	28	N. M.	7.0
Tenn.	33	Idaho	28	R. I.	7.0
Wis.	33	N. Y.	27	Kan.	6.8
Mich.	32	La.	26	Idaho	6.5
Ohio	31	N. J.	26	Fla.	6.3
Tex.	31	W. Va.	26	Mont.	6.1
Ore.	30	Wyo.	25	Ark.	5.9
Vt.	30	Nev.	25	Utah	5.8
W. Va.	30	Mo.	24	Vt.	5.4

Size-Group V.

State	No. of Sen.	State	No. of Com.	State	Size of Com.
Md.	29	N. H.	24	Mich.	5.4
Wyo.	27	Del.	23	Ore.	5.2
N. M.	24	Ariz.	22	Wis.	5.1
N. H.	24	Ohio	21	Del.	5.0
Utah	20	Va.	20	N. H.	5.0
N. J.	19	N. M.	18	Ariz.	4.8
Ariz.	19	Utah	12	Wyo.	4.1
Del.	17	R. I.	11	Nev.	4.0
Nev.	17	Wis.	9	N. J.	3.0

HOUSE

Size-Group IV.

State	No. of Rep.	State	No. of Com.	State	Size of Com.
R. I.	100	N. Y.	33	Md.	9.6
Va.	100	Ill.	32	Colo.	9.5
Wis.	100	N. H.	32	Wash.	9.5
Tenn.	99	N. J.	31	Ky.	9.1
Wash.	97	N. M.	31	Ark.	9.0
Fla.	95	Neb.	30	S. D.	8.6
W. Va.	94	Utah	30	Neb.	8.2
Cal.	80	Nev.	29	Ariz.	7.7
Idaho	68	Okla.	29	Wis.	7.0

Size-Group V.

State	No. of Rep.	State	No. of Com.	State	Size of Com.
Colo.	65	Wyo.	29	Wyo.	7.0
Wyo.	62	W. Va.	28	N. M.	6.8
N. J.	60	Ariz.	27	Utah	6.4
Ore.	60	Del.	27	Idaho	6.3
Utah	55	Vt.	26	Ore.	6.2
Ariz.	54	Va.	25	Mich.	6.2
N. M.	49	S. C.	25	N. J.	5.0
Nev.	37	Wis.	22	Del.	5.0
Del.	35	R. I.	14	Nev.	4.7

there may be committee stationery (appropriately headed so as not to keep the names of the members under a bushel) with postage allowance. Whatever the real reason for their retention, be it sheer inertia or spoils, these barnacles cling tenaciously to the legislative hull. Created presumably to serve the public interest, they remain often to clutter up the scenery and serve the private interests of the members. Defenders of these committees, however, exist. One legislator insisted that they are not "useless" but are highly useful in the legislative process in what he termed a "practical way." As an illustration he cited a case of Johnny Jones, chairman of the Committee on, let us say, Commerce. That committee never receives any bills for consideration. But, Johnny writes to his constituents on committee stationery and, to folks in his end of town, the Committee on Commerce is something of importance. "Look at Johnny," they say to one another; "he's getting on." Incidentally, the advertising doesn't hurt Johnny's insurance business any. All of which is just what Johnny wanted. He wasn't in line for the chairmanship of an active committee, but he reaps the reward in private life of the prestige gained by the chairmanship he received. In payment, he supports the "powers that be" in voting for their legislation. The "useful" purpose is thus attained. The writer did not pause to argue the definition of "useful," nor to suggest the launching of a campaign for more and bigger committees in order that every member might receive the bauble of a committee chairmanship for the glory of the commonwealth!

The growth of committees seems to parallel the growth of administrative agencies in our state governments. Just as a new function of government was wont to produce a new administrative agency, at least until the reorganizers got busy, so a new field of legislation brings about the creation of a new set of committees. The creation of each new hospital for the insane in different sections of Indiana necessitated the creation of a new "insane" board for its governing. The existence of a state institution in Michigan seems to necessitate the existence of a corresponding legislative committee.

Note the names of the following committees in the Michigan House of Representatives: Boys' Vocational School, College of Mines, Girls' Training School, Ionia State Hospital, Kalamazoo State Hospital, Michigan School for the Blind, Michigan School for the Deaf, and on through a list of twenty-seven. To illustrate further the process of addition to committee numbers, it is noted that committees on Aviation or Aeronautics have been created in ten houses and four senates, with the joint rules of two other states making similar provision. In contrast, Pennsylvania still has a senate committee on Canals and Inland Navigation, the Illinois Senate one on World's Fair and the Maryland House one each on Currency and Insolvency.

Attention has already been given to the size of committees in relation to the number of legislators. Further consideration is now due. It should be noted first that there is a very wide range of average sizes in both branches—from 3 to 23 in the senates and from 4.7 to 35.6 in the lower houses. Just what constitutes a "large" committee may be difficult to determine. Congressman Robert Luce writes:

> The common experience of mankind is that boards, trustees, directors—in brief, conferring groups of all sorts—work to best advantage when they comprise from five to fifteen members. A larger number invites the formalities of oratory; may require some elevation of voice; brings the hampering influences of ceremony; discourages candor, frankness, bluntness; lessens the likelihood of attendance and punctuality; and weakens personal interest by diminishing personal sense of responsibility.[55]

Obviously, the size of any particular committee may have to be determined by the particular purposes it is intended to serve. Some committees, for instance, may need to be representative of various sections of the state. Such, particularly, are apportionment committees or those dealing with local legislation. Such representation may increase the committee to a size beyond the ordinary. Again, the location of a particularly important industry may be reflected in the size and personnel of a committee. An illustration is to be seen in Maryland where sixteen counties and Baltimore City

---

[55] Legislative Procedure, p. 130.

border on Chesapeake Bay or contain tributaries of it and are, therefore, interested in the oyster industry. In states where roads and highways are constructed under a scheme of separate legislative authorization, wide representation may be demanded on committees considering such legislation. In fact, if representation rather than expertness be considered the goal of committee composition a larger membership is apt to be the result.

Another cause for large committees, particularly when considered in connection with the size of the houses, would seem to be the desire of the members for an imposing array of assignments. Some legislators, doubtless, do not look unkindly upon the idea of receiving many appointments, merely for the sake of any possible prestige to be derived therefrom. One member is recalled who remarked to acquaintances that both the governor and the speaker thought highly of him and had, therefore, favored him in making up the committees. Although he was of the party opposite to that of the speaker and governor and had been assigned to several inactive committees, the mere number of his committee places pleased him greatly. Other legislators desire a wide committee assignment in order to have a chance to help in the consideration of a greater variety of measures. Whatever the motive, the personal desire for many committee assignments doubtless has its effect upon committee sizes.

There seems, moreover, to be a tendency toward what may be termed a natural growth. In any one session some reason or excuse brings about an addition to the membership of some committees. The following session adopts the committee sizes of the previous session whether the reason longer exists or not and proceeds to add to the size of other committees or perhaps of the same ones over again. The result in any case is the same: committees finally become of such size in some states that the real purposes of committees would seem to be almost, if not entirely, lost. As an extreme example of large committees, attention is called to the Georgia House of Representatives where thirty-five committees have more than twenty-five members each, ten of these having a membership between fifty and seventy-five.

Aside from the difficulties involved in making large committees workable, the fact of large membership combined with that of a large number of committees produces a mechanical difficulty of first rate importance. Each legislator must of necessity sit on many committees. The columns headed " Average Assignments " in Table 2 show the average committee assignments for each member in the various legislative bodies. The average figure does not, of course, tell the whole story. In the South Carolina Senate, where the average number of assignments is 7.3, one individual is found to have fourteen assignments, one thirteen, and one eleven. In the Illinois Senate, showing an average assignment of 18.5, one senator was on thirty-eight committees, two on twenty-nine and one on twenty-eight! The South Carolina House shows a rather low average—2.7—but one member had nine assignments and three had seven each.

It is to be noted that the average assignment throughout the country is 7.6 in the senates and 4.46 in the lower houses. A comparison of the fourth and sixth and of the tenth and twelfth columns indicates a close correlation between large committees and numerous assignments. Of the seventeen senates showing a committee size above the average for all forty-five, fifteen show also a higher assignment than the general average. Of the fifteen senates showing a higher assignment than the general average, thirteen are among those having a larger committee size than the average in the forty-five states. Of the twenty houses whose committee sizes are greater than the general average, nine have also a higher member assignment than the average of the forty-five states. The other eleven states whose house members have committee assignments above the general average, have committee sizes not far below the mean. While the correlation in the houses is below that of the senates, there is seen to be a relationship, certainly largely causal, between member assignments and committee size.

As in the case of committee sizes, it may be difficult to

determine what should be the maximum number of committee assignments. It will, of course, depend on various factors. In the first place, chairmanship of an active committee means, of necessity, a greater amount of work for a legislator than mere membership. It requires also more nearly perfect attendance. A second factor is that of the amount of work assigned to the committee. Membership on some committees is of major importance requiring attendance at frequent committee meetings, while at the other extreme there may be nothing involved save having a committee position attached to one's name. Obviously, if a committee member is to fulfill the duties of his membership, it must be made possible for him to attend committee meetings. But wide membership produces conflicts and necessary non-attendance. Many legislators have expressed the opinion that membership on two active committees is all that any member should have. It would seem possible to add to this, membership on perhaps two less active committees, for instance, one of a formal nature and one which normally receives comparatively few bills. Beyond this, membership will ordinarily necessitate non-attendance, thus defeating the purpose of the committee, or such membership must be on inactive committees and hence more or less useless. The dilemma of numerous committee assignments becomes then apparent—compulsory non-attendance or useless inactivity. A glance at the tables indicates how prevalent the dilemma must be, there being only eight senates out of forty-five where senators average less than five assignments each, while fourteen show a higher average assignment than eight. In the houses, while the average is not so far above the suggested norm, there are fourteen bodies showing an average higher than five for each member, and twenty-four, or more than half, with an average above four, the suggested norm. It should, of course, be noted again that the average is often far below the committee assignments of certain individual members, so that, even where the average is low, some members may face the dilemma cited above.

A comparison of committee assignments in states having

joint committee systems with those in states having a bicameral organization shows a considerable advantage for the
former. As is shown in Table 1, senatorial assignments vary
from 2.3 to 4.5 for each member, with an average in the three
states of approximately 3.4. Table 2 (sixth column) indicates
assignments ranging from 1.5 in the Wisconsin Senate to
18.5 in Illinois with an approximate average of 7.6. This is
almost twice as many as under the joint systems. In the
lower houses, Table 1 shows from 1.5 to 2.1 committee places
for each member, an average of not quite 1.8. The twelfth
column of Table 2 discloses a range of assignments from 1.3
in New Hampshire to 9.2 in Tennessee, averaging approximately 4.5. This is two and-a-half times as many committee
places for each representative as in the states of Table 1.
Only three states with bicameral committees—New Hampshire, Vermont and Wisconsin—have lower average assignments than the general average under the joint committee
systems. Only Rhode Island and Wisconsin have lower
average senatorial assignments than the general average in
the Table 1 states. That a small committee assignment is
possible, however, even with a bicameral organization is
indicated by such states as Idaho, New York, Rhode Island
and Wisconsin.

CHAPTER II

COMMITTEE ORGANIZATION IN MARYLAND AND PENNSYLVANIA

A. Composition of Committees

The General Assembly of Maryland is organized, so far as the committee system is concerned, on a strictly bicameral basis with a single exception. The Constitution prescribes:

a joint standing committee of the Senate and House of Delegates, who shall have power to send for persons and examine them on oath and call for public or official papers and records; and whose duty it shall be to examine and report upon all contracts made for printing, stationery, and purchases for the public officers and the library, and all expenditures therein, and upon all matters of alleged abuse in expenditures, to which their attention may be called by resolution of either House of the General Assembly.[1]

This committee is generally known as the Grand Inquest committee and came into particular prominence in 1929 because of an investigation into the expenditures of the State Roads Commission.

All other standing committees are provided for in the standing rules of the Senate and the House of Delegates. In the former, there are to be twenty-nine committees " appointed at the beginning of each session by the President [2] unless otherwise ordered by the Senate." [3] The number of members on each [4] is designated in the rule and it is further provided that " The first named of every committee shall be chairman." [5] The House rule [6] enumerates thirty-five committees, varying in size from four to twenty, to be appointed by the Speaker. Three further specifications are made concerning committee membership. First, " the Speaker and four other

---

[1] Constitution of Maryland, Art. III, Sec. 24.
[2] Maryland has no Lieutenant-Governor. The President of the Senate is elected by the Senate.
[3] Rules of the Senate of Maryland, 1929, Rule 16.
[4] Varying from three to eleven.
[5] Rule 15, ibid.
[6] Rules of the Maryland House of Delegates, 1929, Rule 44.

members " compose the Rules committee. Second, the Committee on Chesapeake Bay and its Tributaries is to

> . . . consist of twenty members, as follows: One from each of the Legislative Districts of Baltimore City [7] and from each of the following counties [8]: Baltimore, Anne Arundel, Charles, Calvert, St. Mary's. Harford, Cecil, Kent, Queen Anne's, Talbot, Dorchester, Wicomico, Worcester, Somerset, Caroline and Prince George's.

The third specification reads as follows:

> The minority representation on each of the above named committees of the House having fifteen members shall be five, thirteen members shall be four, and on each of said committees having nine members shall be three, except the Committee on Currency, which shall have a minority representation of six members.[9]

A prominent feature of the legislative process in Maryland is the frequent use of local committees. Although these are designated " select " rather than " standing," they attain practically to the latter status. All bills affecting a single county or subdivision thereof, or Baltimore City, are assigned in the House to the county delegation or that of Baltimore City acting as a standing committee for such proposed legislation. Where counties have only two delegates, which is true in six cases, some other delegate is appointed to sit with them on the committee. Ordinarily the same delegate is chosen to sit with a given delegation on each succeeding measure referred. In the Senate, local bills are referred to a " select " committee, composed, in the case of Baltimore City, of the six senators therefrom. In the case of any county measure, the committee consists of the senator from that county acting as chairman, and two other senators, usually, although not always, from nearby counties. It would seem, however, that the added members are of but little significance, the chairman being left to handle the measure to suit himself in large part. In

---

[7] Baltimore City is divided into six legislative districts, which, with the sixteen counties named, gives an actual membership of twenty-two. The rule, however, still reads " twenty."

[8] These counties all border the Chesapeake or contain important tributaries thereof.

[9] Rule 44. The last committee has had no measures referred to it in the last two sessions. Its minority majority was apparently for the purpose, originally, of furnishing the minority party with a committee room and secretarial help. The minority representation was decreased in 1931.

fact, it is doubtful if formal meetings of these senate " select " committees are often held. The importance, however, of local legislation thus handled in the two houses can be appreciated when it is noted that of nine hundred seventy-two commitments in the House of Delegates in the 1929 session, three hundred ninety-two were sent to local delegations. In the Senate, out of eight hundred fifty-eight commitments of bills, three hundred sixty-four were referred to such " select " committees.[10] A study, therefore, of Maryland's committee system would be woefully incomplete without including a view of this practice in respect to local legislation. What this really amounts to is that each delegation in the House of Delegates, from a county or from Baltimore City, is a standing committee. In the Senate, the six senators from Baltimore City act as a standing committee, as does each senator from the twenty-three counties.

Giving attention first to the standing committees as provided in the rules, we have in the accompanying table the size, number of committees of each size, and the total of committee places in the two houses. It is to be noted that the most prevalent size in both the Senate and the House of Delegates is nine, although the former is more given to large committees than the latter. The average size of the twenty-

TABLE 4.   MARYLAND COMMITTEE STATISTICS—1929.[11]

SENATE			HOUSE OF DELEGATES		
Size	Number	Committee Places	Size	Number	Committee Places
3	1	3	4	1	4
5	2	10	5	1	5
7	4	28	9	28	252
8	1	8	11	1	11
9	12	108	13	2	26
11	8	88	15	1	15
12	1	12	22	1	22
Total 29		257		35	335
Joint Com.		5			13
Total		262			348

[10] These "commitments" include joint resolutions, House and Senate bills, and recommitments, if to a different committee than the one first receiving it.

[11] Data in this table and table 6 compiled from printed official lists.

nine Senate committees is eight and eighty-six hundredths; of the thirty-five House committees, nine and fifty-seven hundredths. Such size would not seem to be extreme when considered absolutely, but, relative to the size of the body and the number of committees, it appears differently. The Senate has twenty-nine members, of which the President serves only on the Committee on Rules. Dividing the two hundred sixty-one remaining places among the twenty-eight remaining senators, we have an average committee assignment of nine and thirty-two hundredths for each member. To serve on from nine to ten different committees, in addition to handling one's own local legislation, is asking a good deal, even of a senator. It should be noted here, however, that the seeming burden is considerably lightened by the fact that many of these committees never receive any measures for consideration. In the House of Delegates, with one hundred eighteen members, the Speaker serves on the Rules and Grand Inquest Committees only. The three hundred forty-six committee places, equally divided, would give each member a committee assignment of just less than three. The members, however, do not receive an equal number of assignments, eleven members in the session of 1929 being without committee places entirely, with a corresponding increase in places for other members. Again, as in the Senate, the "local" committees are not included and all "standing" committees are, even though many of them receive no bills.

Any constructive criticism of the committee system must be based, not on a casual view of the size and number existent, but upon the work which these committees perform. What committees may be eliminated? How can the size be adjusted to the task? To what extent do multiple committee assignments overburden some members and leave others with comparatively little committee work? These questions must seek an answer in a study of the work performed by the individual committees. The accompanying table (Number 5) presents a summary view of the number of measures, including joint resolutions and recommittals (to a committee other than the one reporting), referred to each committee in the Senate and

TABLE 5. MEASURES REFERRED TO COMMITTEES, MARYLAND.[1]

SENATE COMMITTEES					HOUSE COMMITTEES				
Com. No.	1927	1929	Total	Per cent.	Com. No.	1927	1929	Total	Per cent.
1	5	6	11	1.1	1	10	17	27	2.3
—					1'	0	7	7	0.6
2	4	9	13	1.3	2	7	6	13	1.1
3[2]	0	2	2	0.2	3[2]	0	6	6	0.5
4	1	0	1	0.1	4	0	0	0	0.0
5	0	0	0	0.0	—				
6	23	10	33	3.3	6	31	8	39	3.4
7	1	29	30	3.0	7	3	6	9	0.8
8	8	13	21	2.1	8	7	21	28	2.4
9	14	8	22	2.2	9	17	11	28	2.4
10[3]	0	0	0	0.0	—				
11	10	6	16	1.6	11	6	8	14	1.2
12	118	126	244	24.4	12	160	168	328	28.5
—					12'	0	0	0	0.0
13	34	23	57	5.7	13	19	29	48	4.2
14	0	1	1	0.1	14	0	0	0	0.0
15	20	12	32	3.2	15	19	7	26	2.3
16	244	229	473	47.3	16	258	268	526	45.7
17	0	0	0	0.0	17	0	0	0	0.0
18	7	3	10	1.0	18	6	3	9	0.8
19	0	0	0	0.0	19	0	0	0	0.0
20*	0	0	0	0.0	20*	0	0	0	0.0
21	0	0	0	0.0	21	0	0	0	0.0
22	0	0	0	0.0	22	0	0	0	0.0
23	0	0	0	0.0	23	0	0	0	0.0
24	0	0	0	0.0	—				
25	0	0	0	0.0	25	0	0	0	0.0
26	5	6	11	1.1	26	0	1	1	0.1
27*	0	0	0	0.0	27*	1	1	2	0.2
28	9	6	15	1.5	28	6	10	16	1.4
29	0	0	0	0.0	—				
30	6	5	11	1.1	30	5	3	8	0.7
—					31	15	0	15	1.3
—					32	0	0	0	0.0
—					33	0	0	0	0.0
—					34	0	0	0	0.0
—					35	0	0	0	0.0
—					36	0	0	0	0.0
—					37	0	0	0	0.0
—					38	0	0	0	0.0
Total	509	494	1003	100.3		570	580	1150	99.9

[1] Data compiled from files in office of Department of Legislative Reference.
[2] Joint Grand Inquest Committee.
[3] Committee on Executive Nominations.

the House of Delegates in the regular 1927 and 1929 sessions. The first column designates the various committees of the Senate in alphabetical order. Corresponding committees of the House are numbered the same in the sixth column. The use of a dash (—) in either of these columns indicates that no corresponding committee exists in the other house. The starred committees are for formal or procedural purposes. The percentage columns are based on the total number of measures referred to the committees in both sessions. This is exclusive, of course, of all "local" legislation.

A summary of this table shows that of the twenty-six Senate committees, excluding those on Rules, Executive Nominations, and Printed Bills, nine have had no measures referred to them during the two sessions; twelve, including the above nine, have each had less than 1 per cent. of all measures, nine have had from 1 per cent. to 3 per cent.; three have had from 3 per cent. to 10 per cent.; while the remaining two—Finance and Judicial Proceedings—have had 24.4 per cent. and 47.3 per cent. respectively, totalling between them more than 71 per cent. of all committals. In the House of Delegates, of the thirty-three committees—excluding those on Rules and Printed Bills—fifteen have had no committals during the two sessions; twenty-one, including these fifteen, have had each less than 1 per cent.; eight from 1 per cent. to 3 per cent.; two from 3 per cent. to 10 per cent.; and the Ways and Means and Judiciary committees 28.5 per cent. and 45.7 per cent. respectively, a total for these two of over 74 per cent. It is to be noticed, moreover, that with few exceptions the relative number of measures referred to any committee remained fairly constant through the two sessions.

With such information at hand we may proceed to consider the matter of individual committee assignments. Without consideration for the relative importance of committees, the following table (Number 6) shows the distribution of committee places in the Maryland General Assembly in the 1929 session. The third and sixth columns indicate the number of senators and delegates, respectively, holding chairmanships and memberships shown in the two preceding columns.

TABLE 6. COMMITTEE POSITIONS, MARYLAND, 1929.

SENATE			HOUSE OF DELEGATES		
Chairman-ship	Member-ship	No. of Senators	Chairman-ship	Member-ship	No. of Delegates
2	9	2	2	3	1
2	8	4[1]	1	7	1
2	7	1	1	5	5
1	10	1	1	4	10
1	9	6	1	3	4
1	8	3	1	2	6
1	7	1	1	1	4
1	6	2	1	0	1
1	0	1[2]		6	1
	12	1		5	7
	9	2		4	13
	8	4		3	25
	7	1		2	19
				1	10
				0	11

[1] One chairmanship here is of the Joint Committee.
[2] The President of the Senate is Chairman of Rules.

If, however, the relative importance of committees is considered, a more accurate picture is obtained. An attempt is
here made to place a quantitative value on the committee
assignments of each legislator. The percentage of all commitments to any committee during the 1929 session—some
changes in membership having occurred since 1927—is used
as a measuring stick to test the relative importance of the
committees. This is not, to be sure, an accurate measure, the
relative importance of bills varying so widely. But, for lack
of something better, it may show some significant relations.
Using the percentage groups as above,[12] a rating is given for
membership in a committee falling within any group somewhat commensurate with the percentages indicated. On this
basis, the committees having no measures receive no rating.
Those having bills up to 1 per cent. are rated with a value of
1, from 1 per cent. to 3 per cent. with a value of 2, from 3 per
cent. to 10 per cent. with a value of 4, and the two major
committees of each house with a value of 35. It is assumed
for sake of comparison that a committee chairmanship is
worth five times as much as mere membership. This is an
arbitrary figure which may or may not approximate the real

[12] See p. 53, above.

worth. But a different relative value would merely increase or decease the deviation between the committee rating of different members without affecting materially their relative position. Applying such a rating to the Maryland senators it is discovered that nine have a rating below 20, two between 20 and 40, eleven between 40 and 60, two between 60 and 80, two between 90 and 100, one of 186, and one of 215. The last two are chairmen of Judicial Proceedings and Finance respectively.

Application of the same scheme of rating to members of the House of Delegates reveals in a way an even greater inequality of assignments. Twenty-seven members receive 0 for a rating being either on no committee at all, which was true in eleven cases, or only on inactive committees. Of the fifty-nine members rated between 1 and 10, forty-eight rank at 5 or below. In other words, seventy-five members of the House—more than five-eighths of all—received committee assignments rated at 5 or below. Three members rated between 11 and 20, seventeen between 31 and 40, ten between 41 and 60, while the chairmen of the Ways and Means and Judiciary committees received 177 and 176 respectively. Some explanation of these wide variations are suggested in the following section.

Committee organization in Pennsylvania presents many contrasts and some similiarities to the Maryland system just described. Rule 23 of the Senate Rules provides for the appointment of thirty-five committees with specified sizes. Save that the first-named member is to be chairman,[13] and the President *pro tempore* is to be *ex officio* a member of all standing committees,[14] no further rules are found respecting committee organization. In the House, Rule 5 places the power to appoint all standing, select, and conference committees in the Speaker's hands " unless otherwise ordered by the House." Forty-three committees are provided for in Rule 27, a committee on Rules of five members plus the Speaker being authorized by Rule 29. As to size, Rule 28 reads:

The several committees shall consist of not less than twenty-five

---

[13] Rule 24, Pennsylvania Legislative Directory, 1929, p. 17.
[14] Rule 23, ibid., p. 16.

members, except the Committee on Appropriations, which shall consist of not less than forty members, and the Committees on:

Education;	Public Health and Sanitation;
Electric Railways;	Public Roads; and
Municipal Corporations;	Ways and Means,

which shall consist of not less than thirty-five members, and the
Committee on Rules, five members.[15]

The outcome of the application of these rules on committee
composition in the 1929 session is shown in Table 7.

TABLE 7.   PENNSYLVANIA COMMITTEE STATISTICS—1929.[16]

	SENATE			HOUSE OF REPRESENTATIVES	
Size	Number	Committee Places	Size	Number	Committee Places
6	1	6	6	1	6
10	1	10	24	2	48
11	2	22	25	15	375
12	2	24	26	2	52
14	2	28	28	2	56
15	5	75	30	2	60
16	2	32	31	2	62
17	3	51	32	3	96
19	6	114	33	1	33
20	1	20	34	2	68
21	2	42	35	2	70
22	2	44	37	3	111
26	1	20	38	2	76
29	2	58	40	2	80
32	1	32	42	1	42
35	1	35	49	1	49
37	1	37	52	1	52
	35	656		44	1336

There is seen to be no particularly prevalent size for Senate
committees although more of them have nineteen members
each than any other size.   The average size of Senate committees is 18.7.   In the House twenty-five is the most prevalent size while the average is 30.4.   These sizes appear to be
large—too large—both absolutely and in' relation to the
legislative membership.   Their large membership makes more
difficult the securing of a quorum, destroys individual responsibility for the consideration of measures, necessitates a

---

[15] Ibid., p. 52.
[16] Data in this and in Table 9 compiled from committee lists in
the Pennsylvania Legislative Directory, 1929.

rather wide use of sub-committees and multiplies individual committee assignments. Pennsylvania Senators, on the average, serve on, or are at least appointed to, more than thirteen committees. Representatives have an average assignment of 6.5. If such committees are at all active, the impossibility of attending all one's committee meetings becomes immediately apparent, particularly in the Senate. If one's committees, on the other hand, are inactive, then they are merely baubles with no proper place in the system.

An analysis, however, of committee assignments must be based, as was done above, on a classification of committees by work assigned. In the accompanying table (Number 8) the House committees are numbered consecutively from 1 to 44, including that on Rules, number 42. Similar Senate committees bear the same numbers with three having no counterpart in the House being added below. One of these is the Committee on Executive Nominations. The second and fifth columns show the number of measures referred to each committee in the 1929 session, including those recommitted, if to a different committee than the one previously in possession of the measure. The third and sixth columns indicate in the respective houses the percentage of all commitments made to each committee. In other words, the percentages for Senate committees is based on a total of 1815 commitments, and for House committees on a total of 2658.

Using the same percentage groups as was done for Maryland, a summary of this statistical material discloses the following:

Senate Committees having no measures					3, totaling	0.0%
"	"	"	each less than 1%		17, "	4.9%
"	"	"	" from 1% to 3%		6, "	9.2%
"	"	"	" " 3% to 10%		5, "	28.1%
"	"	"	" " 10% to 26%		3, "	57.8%
"	"	, total (excluding Rules and Executive Nominations)			34, "	100.0%

House Committees having no measures					6, totaling	0.0%
"	"	"	each less than 1%		17, "	4.6%
"	"	"	" from 1% to 3%		10, "	15.4%
"	"	"	" " 3% to 10%		7, "	40.5%
"	"	"	" " 10% to 21%		2, "	39.5%
"	"	, total (excluding Rules and Compare Bills)			42, "	100.0%

TABLE 8. MEASURES REFERRED TO COMMITTEES, PENNSYLVANIA, 1929.[1]

SENATE COMMITTEES			HOUSE COMMITTEES		
Com. No.	Measures	Per cent.	Com. No.	Measures	Per cent.
—			1	0	0.0
2	6	0.3	2	9	0.4
3	19	1.0	3	23	0.9
4	458	25.2	4	536	20.2
5	19	1.0	5	36	1.4
—			6	0	0.0
7	5	0.3	7	3	0.1
—			8	0	0.0
9	0	0.0	9	0	0.0
—			10	17	0.6
11	27	1.4	11	53	2.0
12	108	6.0	12	208	7.8
13	61	3.4	13	85	3.2
14	32	1.8	14	38	1.4
15	1	0.05	15	6	0.2
16	3	0.2	16	1	0.04
—			17	10	0.4
18	5	0.3	18	6	0.2
19	17	1.0	19	35	1.3
—			20	0	0.0
21	33	1.8	21	46	1.7
—			22	0	0.0
23	0	0.0	23	0	0.0
24	344	19.0	24	243	9.1
—			25	64	2.4
26	7	0.3	26	96	3.6
—			27	7	0.3
28	2	0.1	28	29	1.1
29	1	0.05	29	2	0.1
30	6	0.3	30	4	0.2
—			31	46	1.7
32	11	0.6	32	30	1.1
33	5	0.3	33	9	0.4
34	92	5.1	34	114	4.3
35	6	0.3	35	11	0.4
36	3	0.2	36	1	0.04
37	1	0.05	37	4	0.2
38	39	2.1	38	32	1.2
39	246	13.6	39	514	19.3
40	0	0.0	40	9	0.4
41	123	6.8	41	238	9.0
42	0	0.0	42	0	0.0
—			43	1	0.04
44	125	6.8	44	92	3.5
45	8	0.5	—		
46	0	0.0	—		
47	2	0.1	—		
Total	1815	99.8		2658	100.1

[1] Information compiled from The History of Senate Bills, 1929, and from The History of House Bills, 1929.

Certain contrasts with Maryland at once appear.[17] In the first place, there is much less concentration of commitments; there are fewer wholly inactive committees and the most active ones receive a lower percentage of measures. It is to be noted further that the Appropriations committees receive the greatest number of measures. The Administrative Code of Pennsylvania, while creating a budget system, does not require the introduction of a general " Budget Bill " as the Maryland Constitution provides. Maryland has no Appropriations committees, the " Budget Bill " and supplementary appropriation measures going instead to the committees on Finance and Ways and Means. The Roads committees, too, are of major importance in Pennsylvania, a very large number of measures, many of them local in character, being sent to these committees. In Maryland, on the contrary, any local measures dealing with roads would probably be referred to a local, " select," committee while the control over the state road system is largely in the hands of the State Roads Commission without much legislative interference. Some explanation of the contrasts is also to be found in the fact that while only one judiciary committee exists in each Maryland house, the Pennsylvania Senate has two and the House three.

It is true, on the other hand, that marked inequalities do exist in the importance of committees as measured by the number of measures referred. Three committees in the Senate received 57.8 per cent. of all measures, while eight of them totalled 85.9 per cent. At the other extreme, twenty of the committees received a total of less than 5 per cent. of all measures. In the House, two committees were given nearly 40 per cent. of all measures while nine most active ones received 80 per cent. Twenty-three of the House committees —more than half of the total number—received together less than 5 per cent.

These differences in the relative activity of committees, whether or not accurately measured by the number of commitments, affect in an important way the committee rating

---

[17] See p. 53, above.

of individual legislators. If no consideration be given to such differences of work, the Pennsylvania legislators may be classified as follows:

TABLE 9.   COMMITTEE POSITIONS, PENNSYLVANIA, 1929.

SENATE			HOUSE OF REPRESENTATIVES		
Chairman-ship	Member-ship	No. of Senators	Chairman-ship	Member-ship	No. of Representatives
1	16	1	1	7	5
1	13	11	1	6	25[1]
1	12	7	1	5	13
1	11	12		9	1
1	10	2		8	7
1	9	1		7	45
1	8	1		6	108
	15	1		5	2
	14	1			
	13	4			
	12	2			
	11	6			

[1] Includes the chairman of the Committee on Compare Bills.

Such a listing shows, however, only the *number* of committee assignments. The senator heading the list, with one chairmanship plus sixteen memberships, presided over a third-rate committee, rating being based on measures referred to it. Only twenty-seven measures, or 1.4 per cent. of all commitments, reached it; while the chairman of the Appropriations committee, with 458 measures, or 25.2 per cent. of all to its credit, is to be found in the group of senators having one chairmanship and eleven memberships. The House statistics would indicate the existence of some forty-three members of approximately equal standing at the heads of committees. Of course, nothing of the sort is true. One representative of the first five in the table was chairman of a wholly inactive committee and held no position on any one of the four committees receiving the largest number of measures.

If we apply the rating scheme used for Maryland, however, giving the four classes[18] of committees a membership value

[18] See page 54. Class I in Senate and House includes committees receiving less than 1 per cent. of all referred measures; Class II, from 1 per cent. to 3 per cent., etc.

somewhat commensurate with the number of bills committed
to them, we can arrive more closely at the relative committee
importance of the members. Using a rating value of 1, 2,
6, and 18, respectively, for Classes I, II, III, and IV, with a
chairmanship valued again at five times a membership, the
result is as follows:

SENATE		HOUSE	
Rating	No. of Senators	Rating	No. of Representatives
11 to 20	3	1 to 10	41
21 to 30	1	11 to 20	64
31 to 40	4	21 to 30	40
41 to 50	5	31 to 40	30
51 to 60	9	41 to 50	17
61 to 70	4	51 to 60	7
71 to 80	10	61 to 70	3
81 to 90	6	71 to 80	2
91 to 100	3	110 to 115	2
101 to 110	1		
125 to 150	3		

If the result be compared with the Maryland situation
there is to be noticed a less extreme deviation in rating among
senators, due primarily to the fact that in Pennsylvania
measures are not so concentrated in a few committees. The
discrepancy in committee rating in the House is not so marked
as it was in the Maryland House of Delegates. No representatives received a zero rating—save one who was necessarily
absent from the session—and a much smaller number received
a rating below 10 than in Maryland. On the other hand, no
members rated as high as did the two major chairmen in the
Maryland House. However, the rating scheme does disclose
the existence of 31 members of major committee importance.
Those rated over 40 were either chairmen of relatively important committees or possessed membership above the average
in the major committees. Thus one representative is found
with a rating of 59 but without any chairmanship whatever.
His high rating is explained by membership on both Class IV
and on three Class III committees. Some suggested explana-
tions of these discrepancies will appear in the sections
following.

B.   Selection of Committee Members and Chairmen

The provisions of the rules governing the appointment of
committees have already been cited.[19]   In both Maryland and
Pennsylvania, the presiding officers of both houses are left
fairly free, so far as the rules are concerned, to make up the
committee lists to suit themselves.   Certain limits there are,
to be sure, as for instance the minority representation on
Maryland House committees and the fixed number of members
in both Maryland houses.   The appointing officials of the
Pennsylvania and Maryland senates are on a par, being re-
stricted only in the matter of committee sizes.   The Pennsylvania Speaker, however, appears to be almost without limits
in his committee selections, the minimum size provision being
the only one found in the rules.   Of course, the major factors
controlling the matter of committee selections are quite outside the rules, often quite outside the legislative body itself.
The desires of the members, their previous legislative experience and committee membership, their occupation or geographical location, their political party or factional membership
—all may affect the appointing official in making his selections.
On the other hand, the wishes of the governor, particularly if
he belongs to the party in control of the legislative bodies, the
desires or demands of political bosses, state and local, the
political ambitions of the appointing official, the nature of
important proposed legislation—these and other unmeasurable
influences doubtless have more effect in many cases than do
the more evident factors.

As an illustration of the process of committee selection the
following description related by one presiding officer possesses
merit.   In the first place he asked the members to furnish him
a sheet of paper containing their committee preferences,
reminding them that they could not all receive places on the
very few major committees.   With this information at hand,
with a list of the members showing their previous legislative
and committee experience and with another showing their

---

[19] See pp. 48, 49, 55, above.

geographical location and occupation or profession, he proceeded to make up his committees. The tentative list thus prepared was submitted to the governor for his approval and suggestions. State and local bosses came forward with their ideas. Finally, the roster was complete and, on the next legislative day, was submitted to the chamber.

The relator made no evaluation of the control exercised by the various factors—it would doubtless be quite impossible to do so. But it does appear, even from such a brief sketch, that the process of committee making is a complicated one and further that it is considered an important part of legislative procedure by those directly interested in legislation.

That the requests of members do have some effect upon committee selection is attested by their correlation.[20] In the Maryland Senate and House, certain members both of the majority and minority parties testified that their committee positions tallied very accurately with their requests. The same was found true in the Pennsylvania House of Representatives, no senators in that state having been approached on the subject. However, the fact that certain Maryland delegates were deprived in 1929 of major positions held in 1927 indicates that personal desires must sometimes, at least, give way to other considerations. Further, the very low rating received by some members, particularly of the minority party or of an insurgent faction, as in the Maryland House of Delegates, shows the lack of force in personal committee requests. The twenty-seven Maryland delegates who received a zero committee rating and the forty-eight others who rated at five or below must have either been disappointed in their committee requests or else they showed very poor judgment.

When a comparison is made of the occupation or profession of legislators with their committee assignments, further light is shed upon the process of selection. It may be assumed that, to a certain extent at least, the members made their requests

[20] A majority party senator in Maryland testified, however, that committee appointments depend but slightly upon expressed preferences.

somewhat in relation to their interests. In part the actual committee position seems to agree therewith. The accompanying table shows the occupation or profession of certain committee chairmen in the Maryland General Assembly for 1929. The first part (A) indicates close connection, the second (B) no evident connection at all.

(A) SENATE	
Occupation or Profession	Chairman of Committee
Farmer	Agriculture and Labor
Physician	Sanitary Conditions of the State
Lawyer	Judicial Proceedings
Insurance	Insurance, Fidelity, etc.
Appraiser	Revaluation and Assessment
(B)	
Insurance	Chesapeake Bay (Oysters)
Auctioneer	Elections
Lumberman	Amendments to Constitution

(A) HOUSE	
Occupation or Profession	Chairman of Committee
Farmer	Agriculture
Lawyer	Judiciary
Pharmacist	Hygiene
Lawyer	Amendments to Constitution
(B)	
Canner	Library
Oyster Packer	Education
Contractor and Lumberman	Game and Fish
Dentist	Federal Relation
Lawyer	Chesapeake Bay and Tributaries

In support of the idea that close relationships exist, the only auctioneer in the Senate was on the Committee on Revaluation and Assessment (inactive, to be sure); and the only banker was a member of the Finance Committee. Of six farmers, five were on Agriculture and Labor; and of nine lawyers, all were on Judicial Proceedings; and both physician senators were members of the committee on Sanitary Conditions in the State. In the House five out of nine members of the Agriculture Committee were farmers while all members of the Judiciary committee save one or two were lawyers. It may or may not have any significance—one wonders if this is a little joke perpetrated by the Speaker: the chairman of the committee on Expiring Laws was a funeral director.

A not entirely dissimilar situation is disclosed by the following data on Pennsylvania, the question marks indicating doubt as to close relationship.

(A) SENATE		(A) HOUSE	
Occupation or Profession	Chairman of Committee	Occupation or Profession	Chairman of Committee
Lawyer	Judiciary General	Veterinarian	Agriculture (?)
Lawyer	Repeal Bills	Insurance	Insurance
Insurance	Insurance	Lawyer	Judiciary General
Coal Dealer	Mines and Mining (?)	Lawyer	Judiciary Local
Theatrical Manager	Exposition Affairs (?)	Lawyer	Judiciary Special
(B)		**(B)**	
		Coal Merchant	Banks and Banking
Real Estate and Investment Banker	Agriculture	Farmer	Compare Bills
		Banker	Municipal Corporations
Manufacturer	Judiciary Special	Well Driller	Elections
Iron Master and Farmer	Public Health and Sanitation	Machinist	Game
		Publisher	Mines and Mining
Philadelphia Lawyer	Roads and Highways	Publisher	Public Roads

Most of the large committees in Pennsylvania, however, exhibited a rather thorough mixture of professions. The committee on Agriculture, for instance, consisted of four lawyers, two real estate and insurance men, two publishers, two physicians, and one each of the following: Insurance, Investments, Manufacture, Banker, Undertaker, Teacher, "Retired," and Farmer. There were, however, only two farmers in the Senate.

Evidently the occupational or professional interest of the legislator is not a controlling factor in determining committee assignments. Some effect it has, doubtless, but other factors often overpower it. Of course, in a legislature where most of the work is done by a very few committees regardless of their names, there is slight advantage in a position on a committee which in name alone seems to correspond to one's interest.

A second possible determinant of committee place may be that of previous committee experience. It may be assumed that a legislator will be more familiar with the general type of measures coming before a committee on which he has served than with other measures. He ought therefore to be more efficient if retained on his former committees. Change toward membership on more important committees is nearly always the member's desire. Such change may not necessarily

5

be for the general welfare. Without regard, however, to the desirability or the undesirability of change, it may be possible to measure the extent to which committee assignments in one session follow those of previous sessions. The following tables show this relationship in statistical form, based on committee positions held by members of the 1929 session.

TABLE 10. RELATION OF COMMITTEE POSITION TO PREVIOUS
COMMITTEE EXPERIENCE, MARYLAND.[1]

	SENATE	HOUSE
No. of Committee Places 1929...	245	333
No. of Committee Places 1927...	242	320
No. Repeated in 1929...	235 [2]	248 [2]
No. of Committee Places 1924...	72	92
No. Repeated in 1927...	43	22 [3]
No. of Committee Places 1922...	43	21
No. Repeated in 1924...	21 [3]	8
No. of Committee Places 1920...	20	...
No. Repeated in 1922...	12	...
No. of Committee Places 1918...	13	...
No. Repeated in 1920...	7	...
Total Committee Places held by 1929 members before 1929...	390	433
Total Committee Places repeated in subsequent sessions......	318	278
Percentage of Repetition........	81.5 per cent.	64.2 per cent.

[1] Based on published official lists, 1918-1929.
[2] Same members save for vacancies filled.
[3] New appointing official.

If the number of committee places in 1927 is divided into the number of repetitions of 1927 assignments, the result shows a 97.1 per cent. relation in the Senate, and 77.5 per cent. relation in the House.

Similar statistics for the members of the 1929 Pennsylvania legislature are collected in the following table.

TABLE 11. RELATION OF COMMITTEE POSITION TO PREVIOUS
COMMITTEE EXPERIENCE, PENNSYLVANIA.[1]

	SENATE	HOUSE
No. of Committee Places 1929...	538	904
No. of Committee Places 1927 [2] .	488	796
No. Repeated in 1929...	452	509
No. of Committee Places 1925...	307	516
No. Repeated in 1927...	278	374
No. of Committee Places 1923...	215	303
No. Repeated in 1925...	212	199
No. of Committee Places 1921...	154	165
No. Repeated in 1923...	142	104
No. of Committee Places 1919...	108	132
No. Repeated in 1921...	76	97
No. of Committee Places 1917...	73	71
No. Repeated in 1919...	59	45
No. of Committee Places 1915...	53	52
No. Repeated in 1917...	47	18
No. of Committee Places 1913...	48	43
No. Repeated in 1915...	35	22
No. of Committee Places 1911...	39	26
No. Repeated in 1913...	26	17
No. of Committee Places 1909...	17	11
No. Repeated in 1911...	5	7
No. of Committee Places 1907...	...	7
No. Repeated in 1909...	...	2
No. of Committee Places 1905...	...	3
No. Repeated in 1907...	...	1
No. of Committee Places 1903...	...	4
No. Repeated in 1905...	...	1
Total Committee Places held by 1929 Members before 1929...	1502	2129
Total Committee Places repeated in subsequent sessions......	1332	1396
Percentage of Repetition........	88.7 per cent.	65.6 per cent.
Percentage of Repetition in 1929 of positions held in last previous session in which member served (chiefly 1927).........	92.6 per cent.	63.9 per cent.

[1] Based on committee lists in The Pennsylvania Manual and Smull's
Legislative Handbook.
[2] Includes one Senator and three Representatives as of 1925, because of holding no committee places in 1927.

The above data reveals a very considerable correlation
between committee selections and previous experience. The
correlation would be somewhat increased by considering such
selections as agree with experience in a session or sessions
preceding the most recent one. But it has not been thought
practicable to attempt this. The data used is sufficient to indi-

cate the trend. It is noticed that the percentages in both senates are higher than those in the houses. This may be due to the more stable personnel of the upper houses. Changes seem to be more frequent in early legislative experience, due in part doubtless to the tendency to shift from the less active to the more active committees.

Presumably, a committee member is better fitted for his task by experience in doing it. The repetition of committee assignments therefore would appear to be a healthy tendency. In Maryland one senator is found to have served six sessions on one committee, five sessions on two others, and four on still another three. Another senator has had five sessions' experience on one committee and four on each of two others. A third has been a member of four committees for four sessions, including one chairmanship for the entire period. Two other senators have served through four sessions on two and three committees, respectively. In the House of Delegates, on the other hand, only one member is found to have had as many as four sessions on the same committee and he lost this assignment in 1929. Summarizing the committee experience of the Pennsylvania senators who have had four sessions or more of membership on one or more committees, the following cases of long continued committee service are found: five cases of ten sessions' experience on one committee, eleven of nine, eighteen of eight, fifteen of seven, twenty-two of six, sixty-eight of five, and fifty-seven of four. The two most outstanding examples among the senators show repetition of committee assignments during their legislative careers thus: (1) ten sessions on five committees, nine on two, eight on two, seven on one, six on one, five on three, and four on one; (2) nine sessions on four committees, eight on two, seven on one, and five on four. The record in the house discloses one case of thirteen sessions' experience, one of ten, two of nine, six of eight, six of seven, twenty-nine of six, twenty-six of five, and one hundred ten of four. The most extreme instance is that of a representative with thirteen sessions' membership on one committee, ten on one, eight on one, six on one, five on three, and four on one, disregarding, as has been done throughout this paragraph, those committees which claimed a member for less than four sessions during his legislative career. The discrepancy between Maryland and Pennsylvania in these statistics can be chiefly explained by the fact that in the latter state continued reelections to the legislature are far more frequent than in the former.

Another phase of this same correlation is that of committee chairmanships. No attempt is made to discover the extent to which the rule of seniority is followed. But an examination of the previous experience of committee chairmen in the 1929 sessions discloses some interesting facts. Among Maryland senate chairmen, two had served two sessions each on the committee before becoming its chairman, and two others one session each. The other twenty-six assumed the position with no previous service on the committee. In this last group was the chairman of the highly important Finance Committee, who had, however, served as chairman and member of other committees for three sessions. In the House of Delegates, seven chairmen had previously served for one session each on their respective committees. The other twenty-nine began their committee service as chairmen. Among these was the chairman of the Ways and Means Committee.

The Pennsylvania situation is more easily put into tabular form, the first column showing the number of sessions of service on a committee before attaining the chairmanship.

TABLE 12. PREVIOUS COMMITTEE EXPERIENCE OF CHAIRMEN.

No. of Sessions	Senators	Representatives
8	0	1
7	1	0
6	1	0
5	0	2
4	2	2
3	0	4
2	5	5
1	11	5
0	15	24

Here again, as in Maryland, some of the most important committees are headed by newcomers. The committees on

Finance, Elections, Public Health and Sanitation, and Law and Order in the Senate; on Public Health and Sanitation, Elections, Judiciary Special, Judiciary Local, and Ways and Means in the House are to be found in this list. However, these being important committees, the chairmen have always had experience elsewhere, usually as chairmen of some other committees. Be that as it may, it can hardly be said that the seniority rule in its strictest form has much applicability in either of the legislatures studied.

A third and important factor in the composition of committees is that of politics. Much, perhaps most, of the political significance of committee selections is hidden from view. There are, however, certain facts to be disclosed by an analysis of appointments made. Using the data cited above [21] the relative importance of committee assignments to members of various political groups can be computed. In the Maryland General Assembly two divisions of members may be noted: (1) into a Democratic majority and a Republican minority; (2) into a " regular " and an " insurgent " majority group in the House of Delegates. The Pennsylvania division shows only a Republican majority and a Democratic minority in both houses. The number of members constituting each group is shown in parentheses.

TABLE 13. COMMITTEE RATING OF POLITICAL GROUPS.

	MARYLAND		PENNSYLVANIA	
	Senate	House	Senate	House
General Average Rating.	52.0 (28)	14.0 (118)	64.7 (49)	24.3 (206)
Majority Party Average Rating	60.8 (20)	15.2 (82)	66.2 (43)	25.3 (190)
Minority Party Average Rating	30.0 (8)	11.6 (36)	54.5 (6)	11.4 (16)
Majority Party Average Rating (Regulars)..		18.2 (67)		
Majority Party Average Rating (Insurgents)		1.2 (15)		

It will be noticed that the majority members in the Maryland Senate rate twice as high as the minority members. In

[21] See pp. 54, 55, 61, above.

the House they rate 31 per cent. higher. If only the "regular" Democrats in the House are considered, their rating is 56.9 per cent. higher than the Republican members. In the Pennsylvania Senate the majority members rate only 21.4 per cent. higher than those of the minority but in the House about two and-a-fourth times as high. It is not contended that the political differences are the sole causes of these committee discriminations. A certain part of the difference is accounted for by the fact that committee chairmanships belong almost exclusively to the majority party. This is to be expected. But, beyond the effects of this practice, it seems logical to assume that political groupings are responsible for a major portion of the difference in committee rating. Particularly was this the case in the assignments given, or rather withheld, from the " insurgent " group in the Maryland House of Delegates. These members were rather above the average in length of legislative service and committee experience. But their rating in the 1929 session was practically negligible, ten of them receiving no assignments at all and the others only very minor ones. The attention paid to factions is illustrated by a statement from one presiding officer. Quite frankly and directly he put the idea: " One must have at least one committee composed of 'muldoons' in whose hands proposed legislation will be *safe*." [22]

---

[22] For discussions of the subject matter of this chapter in other States, see particularly Frank E. Horack, " The Committee System " in Statute Law-Making in Iowa, pp. 559-560; Leonard D. White, " Our Legislative Mills; The Legislative Process in Illinois" in National Municipal Review, XII, 716; H. W. Dodds, Procedure in State Legislatures, ch. iv; Kentucky Efficiency Commission, The General Assembly, Pamphlet VI. A general discussion of committee selection is to be found in ch. v of Robert Luce's Legislative Procedure.

CHAPTER III

COMMITTEE PROCEDURE IN MARYLAND AND PENNSYLVANIA

A. Reference of Measures

As has been suggested in previous connections, control over the reference of measures may have considerable influence in determining the final action upon them. An illustration in point is found in the 1929 Maryland Senate. The " Baltimore Amusements Home Rule Bill " had passed the House of Delegates. In the Senate it received a double reference—to the City Senators and to the committee on Judicial Proceedings. The former committee reported it favorably within a very short period of time. But the latter committee kept the bill until final adjournment despite all the parliamentary tactics of its proponents to bring it before the Senate for a vote. A still better illustration is that of House Bill No. 85 in the 1929 Maryland Senate. That bill was referred to the Senate Finance committee which decided upon an unfavorable report. Before the report came back to the Senate, however, a member of the City Senators' group asked the Finance chairman to have the bill re-referred, contending it really belonged to the City Senators. Thereupon the Finance committee reconsidered its former action and reported the bill without recommendation. It was then referred to the City Senators who reported it favorably. The Senate accepted the report and the bill passed without a dissenting vote.

The rules of order in the legislatures studied make provision for reference of measures as follows:

Maryland Senate

Upon the introduction of each Bill or Joint Resolution it shall be read the first time and then referred by the President to its appropriate committee, unless otherwise ordered.[1]

---

[1] Rule 21, Sec. 5, pp. 11-12, Rules of the Senate of Maryland, 1929.

Rule 23 provides similarly for House Bills reaching the Senate.

Maryland House of Delegates

Upon the introduction of each bill or joint resolution, it shall be read the first time and then referred by the Speaker to its appropriate committee unless otherwise ordered.[2]

Pennsylvania Senate

Every bill and joint resolution which may be received from the House of Representatives, or which may be read by a Senator in his place, shall, immediately after being presented to the chair, be referred by the President to the appropriate committee, unless otherwise ordered.[3]

Pennsylvania House of Representatives

No bill shall be considered unless referred to a committee, returned therefrom, and printed for the use of the members, as required by the Constitution, Art. III, Sec. 2.[4]

Bills shall be introduced by filing with the Chief Clerk to be by him numbered and handed to the Speaker for reference to appropriate committees, and report at the session following the day of presentation.

If the Speaker shall neglect or refuse to refer any bill or bills, (whether House or Senate) within two days after presentation, in which the House is in session, it shall be in order for any member to move for the reference of said bill or bills to the appropriate committee or committees. Upon instruction so given, the bill or bills shall be immediately referred to said committee or committees.[5]

With the exception of the special provision in the Pennsylvania House in the last paragraph quoted, these provisions are quite the same as are to be found generally in American legislatures. In practice, the "unless otherwise ordered" clause doubtless has but little importance. Conceivably, the Pennsylvania Senate might use it occasionally if the Lieutenant-Governor belonged to a group different from the one in control. But in the other chambers a motion to change a reference made by the presiding officer would have but slight chance. Having elected him, a majority would be likely to vote to sustain his reference, particularly since most of them

---

[2] Rule 35, p. 14, Rules of the Maryland House of Delegates, 1929.
[3] Rule 31, p. 18, Pennsylvania Legislative Directory, 1929.
[4] Rule 35, p. 54, ibid. This rule applies also to the Senate. See Rule 37.
[5] Rule 17, p. 49, ibid.

would probably have no, or very slight, knowledge of the nature of the bill in question. In practice the advice of the majority floor leader is often sought, or offered, in determining what reference to make. Certainly the desire of the introducer of the measure is sometimes considered. A case is recalled in the Pennsylvania Senate where a bill prohibiting the construction of dams of more than a stated maximum height was referred to the committee on Printing. The explanation of such a curious reference seemed to be the fact that the author wanted to superintend the progress of his bill and hence had it referred to the committee of which he was chairman.

It is undoubtedly true that the vast majority of bills are sent to " appropriate " committees. Whether these are, however, the *most* appropriate may often raise serious doubts. To legislative presiding officers, " appropriate " often means " having some connection with." If called upon to defend their references, they might often be hard-pressed. But whether " appropriate " or not, there is a marked tendency, particularly in Maryland, to assign a major portion of the non-local bills to one of two committees in each house.[6] The existence in Pennsylvania of Appropriations committees, in addition to Finance and Ways and Means, and the division of the normal work of judiciary committees among three in the House and two in the Senate, aid materially in preventing such a concentration of measures as is found in Maryland. On the other hand, the Maryland budget system leaves far less for the legislative finance committees to work on than is true in Pennsylvania.

The marked inequalities of distribution, as evidenced by the data in preceding tables,[7] tend to produce rather obvious results. While most of the committees busy themselves with affairs of state after the fashion of the Council of New Amsterdam in *Knickerbocker's History of New York,* a few are so burdened with a multiplicity of measures as to make due consideration of them impossible. The end-of-the-session

---

[6] See Table 5, p. 53, above.   [7] See pp. 53 and 58, above.

rush is not then confined to the chambers themselves; the same situation is likely to occur in the major committees. This is evidenced by the fact that on the two days next preceding the date of adjournment, the Judicial Proceedings committee of the Maryland Senate reported sixty-four bills out of a total of ninety-two from all the standing committees. Twenty-three others came from the Finance committee leaving only five to be reported by all other committees. A comparable situation existed in the House of Delegates where, out of ninety-one measures reported in the last three legislative days, forty-eight came from the Judiciary committee, twenty-four from Ways and Means and nineteen from all others. These statistics, to be sure, do not include whatever other measures the respective committees chose not to report.

It would be quite impossible to measure quantitatively the extent of improper or questionable references. Assuming, however, that committees are created to consider measures lying within a certain field of legislation, we find many instances of doubtful reference. For instance, in the Pennsylvania House of Representatives fifty-two measures were returned to the House by the committees receiving them, for re-reference. No numbers are, of course, available for bills which should have been returned but were not. A second test of doubtful reference is afforded by consideration of duplicate bills. In 1927 there were introduced in the Maryland General Assembly fifty-one pairs—identical Senate and House Bills. Of these, in nineteen cases, both bills reached the Senate. Out of the nineteen referred in the Senate five House Bills went to committees different from those receiving the identical Senate Bills. Thirty-six pairs were referred in the House. Of these in six cases, the committee reference was different. Similar statistics in the 1929 session show four cases of different reference out of twenty-two chances in the Senate, and five cases out of twenty-four in the House.[8]

The 1927 Maryland House of Delegates furnishes a notable instance of references, difficult to explain by any generally

[8] For further comparisons, see ch. vi.

accepted purposes of committees. The committee on Internal Improvements received fifteen House Bills for considera
tion. The subject matter of these measures is indicated
briefly in the following list:

BILL NUMBER	REPORT	SUBJECT
102, 154, 159, 160..	Favorable	Garrett County Officers.
133................	Amended	Alleghany County Fire Cos.
166................	Favorable	Alleghany County State Attorney
167, 168..........	Favorable	Crisfield (Somerset Co.) Bonds
310................	Favorable	Name of Creek in Anne Arundel Co.
163................	No report	Attachment for wages
346................	No report	Chesapeake Bridge Co. Charter
348................	Favorable	Sale of Tobacco Leaf
398................	No report	Railroads
400................	Favorable	Mine Foreman
415................	Amended	Inter-racial Commission

These references cannot be explained by geographical considerations, the chairman of the committee being from St.
Mary's County, no members being from Garrett, Anne
Arundel or Somerset County, and only one from Alleghany.
Certainly the subject matter has no general close relationship
to the nature of the committee. Neither is there evident any
desire to sidetrack the measures since twelve of them were
reported either favorably or with amendments. But whether
or not an explanation is readily available, the fact remains
that the bills were so referred. Other specific instances are
numerous. Bills to abolish capital punishment, to provide
for the election of members of the Public Service Commission,
to regulate the speed of motor vehicles in Washington County,
to abolish the Board of Police Examiners for Baltimore City
(a political measure), all were sent to the Maryland House
Committee on Ways and Means in 1929. Twelve other bills
relating to the method of appointment of various administrative officers were sent to the same committee. A bill to
regulate Building and Loan Associations, one making certain
roads into boulevards under the traffic rules, and a resolution
to provide for a constitutional amendment (there being a
committee on Amendments.to the Constitution),—these were
referred to the Judiciary committee. Another, granting Baltimore City " Home Rule " in matters of Sunday amusements,

was sent to the Rules committee, the Speaker-author being chairman thereof.   In the Senate a bill to repeal a " Jim Crow " law was referred to the committee on Corporations.

One last indication of the uncertainties of reference is to be seen in the history of Pennsylvania Bills.   The two houses have in large part identical committees—the additional ones in either house are of slight importance except for those committees on " Judiciary, Local " and " Manufacturers."   Even so, seventy-one Senate bills and two hundred seventy-three House Bills were referred to different committees in the second house from that in the house of origin.   It appears that, of the above House bills, one hundred thirty-four were sent to House committees having no Senate counterpart. Assuming that forty per cent. of these (the approximate general average) reached the Senate, there remain still two hundred eighteen out of eight hundred fifty House bills reaching the Senate, more than one-fourth, which received there a reference different from that in the House.   While other evidences of doubtful reference can be easily found, these are sufficient to show how uncertain a procedure it is and how politically wise for a member to be on good terms with the presiding officer.

B.   COMMITTEE MEETINGS

So far as official, published rules are concerned there is little either in Maryland or Pennsylvania concerning committee meetings.   Senate Rule 18 and House Rule 31 in Maryland provide that " No committee shall sit during the sitting (session) of the House (Senate) without special leave." [9]   The Pennsylvania House Rule is almost identical.[10] In the Senate there appears only the following rule:

Every member of a committee shall attend the call of the chairman, . . . ; and in case of his neglect to call the committee together or in case of his absence by sickness or other cause, the committee shall attend the call of the next person named on the committee.[11]

[9] 1929, Senate Rules, p. 9; House Rules, p. 12.
[10] Rule 32, Pennsylvania Legislative Directory, 1929, p. 53.
[11] Rule 24, Pennsylvania Legislative Directory, 1929, p. 17.

It is assumed, at least publicly, in both legislatures, that a meeting cannot be held without a quorum present and that some sort of notice to the members is necessary. But the above rules are the only ones governing the calling or conduct of meetings.

The practice followed in the matter of meetings was observed in both legislatures on various occasions during the 1929 sessions. Although the meetings, excluding public hearings, tend to be closed to the public, certain observations can be made from the outside. Place, time, and method of calling may all have their effect upon committee attendance and hence upon committee product.

With regard to committee rooms, it was found that the major committees in both Senate and House in Maryland had special rooms assigned. In some cases two or more committees were obliged to use the same room, but, since these were not major committees, the danger of conflict was slight. No such definite room assignment was found in either house in Pennsylvania. An occasion is recalled when the members of so important a committee as that on Judiciary General (Senate), did not know, five minutes before the scheduled time, where the committee was to meet. In the House on one occasion, announcements were made of three committee meetings for the same room at the same time. Legislators were to be seen constantly about the halls looking for their committees. A resolution passed the House on April 18, 1929, looking to better room arrangements for 1931.

Time schedules for committee meetings were rare in both states, the only two committees found having a definite and regular time for meeting being the Finance and the Judicial Proceedings committees in the Maryland Senate. In these two cases it must be further stated that they rarely, if ever, met on schedule. Generally, the committees met upon call of the chairman, sometimes with notice of several days, sometimes of twenty-four hours, sometimes of only a few minutes. No evident attempt was made to avoid conflicts between committees with overlapping memberships. One of the Pennsylvania House chairmen stated that conflicts in committee meetings were frequent. As an illustration of such conflicts an analysis is here made of the House committees announced to meet one afternoon *at the same hour.* Comparing the membership of these seven committees, the following interesting conflicts are discovered.

Total number of committee places........................... 240
Number of members holding these 159
Number of members with one committee to attend.......... 98
Number of members with two committees to attend......... 45
Number of members with three committees to attend........ 14
Number of members with four committees to attend......... 2

Had these members all been present and rightly distributed it would have been possible to obtain a 66 per cent. attendance upon all committees. Without such perfection, however, it seems likely that no quorum was present in some of these committees at the appointed hour. For appearance sake, it is of course, possible to be present long enough at two or three meetings to be counted as present and help make up a quorum. Such is not an uncommon practice. An incident is recalled of a member's standing in the open doorway between two committee rooms ready to answer to roll call in both. In the Maryland Senate there were frequent conflicts between the City Senators, the most important of the " select " (local) committees, and the Finance or Judicial Proceedings committee. In such cases the member attended whichever one he chose, or perhaps spent part time at each.

Where no definite schedule exists—and this is generally true as noted above—committees meet at call of the chairmen. No provisions exist in the rules of any of the four houses studied as to how notice of the meeting is to be given. Various practices were discovered. The Pennsylvania House had a large bulletin-board on which many, but by no means all, notices of committee meetings were written. The Senate had a similar board but it seemed to have fallen into disuse. Early in the session notices of meetings were posted near the Reading Clerk's desk in the Maryland Senate but it too ceased to be enlightening as time went on. In all four houses, meetings were often announced at the close of a session either by the committee chairman or by the clerk. Many members had often already left the hall; the notice was sometimes read just after adjournment amidst the confusion of departure; the details of the notice were not always too carefully noted by the clerk who read it. One chairman said that a member must be on the alert to get announcements of committee meetings. Sometimes metings were held without the formality of a public notice, the members being rounded up either by the chairman himself, the committee clerk, or by individual members. Whether in all of such cases an actual quorum was obtained or whether some members were sometimes purposely omitted, no data is available. Certainly, from surface appearance, this is the least defensible of any of the methods named.

Nor was any general practice discovered as to length of notice. In certain cases, notice was published nearly a week in advance. The Pennsylvania House bulletin-board very often carried notices twenty-four hours in advance of the meeting. But many instances were found of announcements at the close of a session for meetings to be held immediately. One announcement was witnessed of a meeting called for a five-minute recess, at least one member of the committee having left the Senate chamber just before announcement was made. It would seem desirable, the action of the committee being of such great importance in determining the final action of the chamber, that announcement be made in such manner as to insure every member's being informed without undue effort on his part. Certainly, the more or less haphazard methods witnessed make sure of no such thing.

It would be practically impossible to determine with any accuracy the relation of the above elements of time, place and method of calling meetings to attendance upon them. Neither has any thorough study been made of committee attendance. The illustrations here given are therefore not cited as typical, although no special evidence appeared that they were unusual. In one meeting of each of four of the more important committees of the Pennsylvania House the following attendance in percentage of total membership was noted at the beginning of business: 30, 42, 43, and 53 per cent. As the meetings went on these percentages increased to 55, 72, 60 and approximately 60 per cent. respectively. It will be noticed that three of these started business without a quorum. One important Senate committee of twenty-eight members began the consideration of bills with only six members present, that number increasing to thirteen after forty-five minutes. The Maryland committees, being markedly smaller than those of Pennsylvania, seemed to show a slightly better attendance. No cases were found of less than a quorum although such may easily have happened. A major Senate committee of eleven members sat through an extended meeting, with important legislation pending, and with a maximum attendance of six senators. It might well be argued that such lack of attendance is not surprising considering the known habits of attendance of legislators upon chamber sessions. But, if the action of the committee is to be generally accepted on the ground that the bill has been adopted by a majority of the select group intended to study it, committee attendance becomes much more important than chamber attendance.

Marked contrast was found in the two states respecting promptness of committee meetings. So far as observed, both Senate and House committees in Pennsylvania were called to order promptly at the appointed time. In Maryland, on the contrary, no instance is recalled of a committee meeting promptly. It was often necessary to hunt around the halls and lobbies to secure enough members for a quorum even at a time long after the announced meeting hour. In numerous cases no meeting was held because of small attendance. The effect of this tardiness, or lack of attendance so as to prevent a meeting, was either less thorough examination of measures because of haste, or delayed action thereon. Committees were forced to adjourn hurriedly so that the Senate and House sittings might begin. Bills awaiting advancement on the calendar were postponed until a later committee meeting could act; or they were hurriedly reported in a condition not even desired by the committee.

Methods of committee consideration are varied. There is a widely prevalent use of sub-committees in both houses in

6

Pennsylvania. They are almost unknown in Maryland. The contrast is doubtless caused in part by two factors: larger committees and a greater number of bills to each committee in the former state.[12] In some committees the chairman seemed to dominate, the members largely acquiescing. In others, he appeared in the role of a presiding officer only, leaving motions, suggestions and debate to the members. He occupied a position somewhere between these two extremes in most committees but with no standardization. In large part, the meetings seemed to be very informal. Debate was carried on, if at all, in more or less of a conversational method, speechmaking being rare. In fact, the amount of committee discussion on measures is, to the uninitiated, surprisingly little. One is inclined to say that, generally, bills are handled by unanimous consent. Out of twenty-six bills considered at one meeting of a major Pennsylvania committee not more than two brought forth any discussion further than a brief explanation. The chairman and four or five members—out of twenty-two present—did practically all the talking. At the rate of one bill every three minutes, the twenty-six measures were either indefinitely postponed, deferred, sent to a sub-committee, or ordered reported favorably. No amendment was offered to any bill and an exceedingly small number of negative votes were cast against any motion. In one case the motion for a favorable report was carried with the understanding that the bill was to be recommitted after second reading for further consideration. Such recommitment was apparently largely a matter of form, the House asquiescing in a motion to recommit made by the committee member reporting the measure.

Somewhat similar procedure was witnessed in a meeting of one of the major Senate committees. Thirteen measures were disposed of in forty minutes. Of these, four were reported by some one senator acting as a sub-committee, his report being accepted as the committee action. Members of the

---

[12] Two committees in each Maryland chamber did, however, receive a very large number of bills. But sub-committees were infrequent even in these.

House appeared in two cases to explain their bills and a senator, not on the committee, in a third case. Representatives of interest-groups appeared in four cases to plead for or explain the bills under consideration. Some bills were deferred without action, some ordered reported favorably, some indefinitely postponed. But, at the rate of a bill every three minutes, the committee did its work. There was very little argument—almost none. A brief explanation in some cases, one man's expression of opinion in others, sufficed as a basis for action. It is often stated in defense of rapid committee action that the members have already considered the bills outside the committee room and discussed them sufficiently to know how to vote. But it was evident, in both committees cited, that the members generally knew nothing of the content of most of the bills before the committee met. Their consent to the action of the committee depended apparently upon their confidence in the man making the suggestion for whatever action was taken.

The procedure in the above two committees seemed to be largely duplicated in other Pennsylvania committees visited. In Maryland, save that sub-committees are much less common, debate and deliberation upon measures were not different from the above. Where measures of particular importance arose, there was doubtless considerable discussion outside the committee room. Where politics was affected, committee members doubtless listened to political advice. But on the vast majority of measures, committee action was a matter of unanimous consent, with but little debate and with weak opposition. The most marked example of extended discussion noted in either state was on a wild-turkey bill, where one of the chief points at issue was whether a gobbler's whiskers could be seen with the bird in flight.

The method of voting in committees was varied and uncertain. Occasionally, the roll of the committees was called and the ayes and noes counted. Sometimes a *viva voce* vote sufficed. Frequently no vote was asked for, the chairman designating the proposed action "if there is no objection." No case is recalled among those witnessed in which any care was taken to record votes for and against. One Maryland chairman, however, stated that on important measures, he always asked the majority to initial the report. It is assumed that, on measures showing close division of the committees, the voting may have been done more carefully.

C. Committee Hearings

No rules exist in either house in Maryland and Pennsylvania touching upon the matter of committee hearings. Everything connected with them is apparently left entirely in the hands of the individual committees. No uniformity was observed in the practice of holding hearings, either as to reason for granting, amount of notice, or method of announcement. Sometimes they were granted upon the request of some interest-group or groups, private or public. Sometimes, apparently, the hearing was held upon the desire of the members of the committee to hear the measure discussed by interested parties. Sometimes it even appeared that the hearing was granted either as a mere gesture, a decision to kill the measure having been already reached, or as a means of justifying its action, the committee having already decided in favor of the bill. Announcements of hearings were sometimes made three weeks in advance, sometimes only a few days. In one case in Maryland, a hearing was granted, but only twenty-four hours were allowed to the proponents of the bill to collect their representatives and material. There was in neither legislature any prescribed method for giving publicity to such hearings, the bulletin-board notices and chamber announcements being used as in the matter of committee meetings. Insufficient as such methods are in informing committee members, they are, of course, wholly inadequate in informing the public. The responsibility for becoming informed on such matters seemed to rest generally upon the parties interested rather than upon the committee although one chairman testified that he usually informed both opponents and proponents of a scheduled hearing if he knew who they were. Those interest-groups employing a legislative agent at the capitol, had therefore, a considerable advantage over groups lacking such a source of information.

In the conduct of the hearings themselves, there was also great variation. Nearly every hearing attended in Pennsylvania began promptly at the appointed hour. Nearly every one attended in Maryland opened a half-hour, an hour, or more, late. Usually the delay was caused by lack of attendance of the committee members themselves. Twenty-six women delegates of welfare organizations sat and stood in a crowded committee room on one occasion for more than a half-hour after the announced time of the hearing before a sufficient number of committeemen appeared to justify the chairman in calling the meeting to order. Some of the absent or tardy members were unavoidably detained by an important game of cards in an adjoining room. Attendance by committee members varied but appeared on the whole to be less regular than upon meetings. Somewhat of their attitude was reflected in a remark of one legislator when complaint was made that no quorum was present to open the hearing: " You don't have to have a quorum," he said; " this is only a hearing." Very often less than half the members of a committee would be in attendance, although in certain cases interest was keen and attendance well up toward the full membership. The nature of the bill or bills under consideration, the character of the proponents or opponents, possible conflicts with meetings of other committees, the state of mind of the individual committeeman—these factors, and doubtless others, affected attendance upon hearings.

In general, it must be said, however, that the attitude of the committees toward people appearing before them was very fair. Only one instance is recalled of what appeared unfair treatment. One Maryland Senate chairman displayed what might best be described as a belligerently antagonistic attitude toward the parties presenting one side of the case. Usually, attention (of those in attendance) was good and questions were asked in a respectful manner. It was to be noted that committee members were rarely to be seen making any memoranda of information offered. Since no stenographic record of the hearings was kept in either legislature, the value of a few notes would seem obvious.

Public attendance upon these hearings is largely confined to a few groups. The general public is not represented unless it may be by the committee itself. But official groups come— state administrative officers, representatives of local governments and members of special commissions which have perhaps prepared and sponsored the measure. The appearance before the committees of these official groups, particularly the administrative officers, seems to be of particular significance. As will be pointed out in a later connection, a considerable share of legislation originates with these same official agencies. Their representatives then appear before committee meetings or hearings to explain desires and urge committee action. Sometimes they come of their own volition. Often they are invited by the committee or its chairman to appear for questioning or discussion. Observation indicated that, in Pennsylvania particularly, there was rather close relationship between the legislative committees and the administrative officers. Statements from committee chairmen and from officials in the departments substantiate the idea. The legislative representative of one Maryland department said that the chairman of the corresponding Senate committee brought all bills to him for advice and referred to the House committee chairman as being " very co-operative." It was found that many executive departments located in Baltimore maintained a representative in Annapolis during the session to look after the bills in which the department was interested. Thus is " separation of powers " maintained!

But the official groups are not alone in making their appearance at committee meetings and hearings. Social welfare groups also come, to urge upon the committees their reasons for various proposed social legislation. Most of all, the private interest-groups come—representatives of chambers of commerce, of labor unions, of medical societies, of hotel-keepers' associations, of coal-mine operators, etc.,—each group, of course, arguing that what it proposes to have done or not done will be for the best interests of the commonwealth. How much effect these hearings have upon the ultimate action of the committee is problematical. There appears to be a good deal of wasted effort. However, many legislators have insisted that public hearings have often had the effect of changing enough votes in a committee to change a minority into a majority. The most efficient method, probably, of accomplishing the same result is the one employed by legislative agents everywhere—" bringing pressure to bear." This pressure is more often applied privately and may vary with the individual legislator, the nature of the measure and the character of the legislative agent. The hearing, however, still appears valuable enough as an instrument in determining legislation to induce the Pennsylvania Chamber of Commerce to urge attendance upon certain public hearings in which business was directly interested. On the other hand, several legislators interviewed on the subject insisted that valuable information was often obtained.

It should not be assumed that hearings are always granted upon request. On the contrary, the committee, or its chairman, exercises independent judgment, granting or denying hearings with changing circumstances. No data exist to indicate the relative proportion of hearings granted and denied. And without some knowledge of the importance and merit of the measures concerned, such data would mean but little even if compiled. It would seem, however, that so long as some interest-groups have access to the legislators through permanent legislative agents, other groups should have a chance, at least on important measures, to air their views before the committee in a public hearing.[18]

---

[18] Committee procedure in other States is described in Horack, pp. 563 ff.; Dodds, ch. iv; A. C. Hanford, " Our Legislative Mills: Massachusetts Different from the Others," in National Municipal Review, XII, 42-43; and in O. K. Patton, " Methods of Statute Law-Making in Iowa," in Statute Law-Making in Iowa, pp. 217 ff.

CHAPTER IV

COMMITTEE CONTROL IN MARYLAND AND PENNSYLVANIA

Since the committees act, at least in theory, as agents of the legislative chambers, it seems quite logical that certain methods of control should exist. In an earlier chapter there was a discussion of the various rules existing in various state legislatures to this end.[1] The mere existence of rules, however, may have but slight effect upon actual practice. It therefore becomes necessary to examine not only the rules, but also their application, and further legislative practice in matters of committee control which are not covered by formal rules.

A. COMMITTEE RECORDS

No rule exists in either of the Maryland houses nor in the Pennsylvania Senate respecting the keeping of any records by the committees. In these three houses therefore our study must be confined to the practice alone. Rule 31 of the Pennsylvania House of Representatives reads as follows:

Each of said committees shall keep a record or minute of all proceedings before them, which record or minute shall be open for examination by any member of the House or Senate, or upon leave granted by the respective committee to any one. The committee records shall be filed with the Resident Clerk, upon the final adjournment of the House, to be kept for a period of two years.[2]

This rule was adopted in the 1923 session so as to provide a record of committee activity not theretofore available. In application, however, the rule is not all it seems to be. The "record or minute of all proceedings" consists in practice of something like the following: attendance of members; number and title of bills received; date of receipt; date and nature of committee action. No record of ayes and noes is kept, but merely the general statement that the committee has taken one action or another. No one apparently ever asks to inspect

---

[1] Ch. i, pp. 19-26.
[2] Pennsylvania Legislative Directory, 1929, p. 53.

the committee record. The filing provision of the rule is wholly disregarded, some committee chairmen being unaware of its existence. A request to the Resident Clerk for records of a previous session disclosed the fact that he had no knowledge of his duty under the rule, no records ever having been filed.

The result of the above rule is thus no more than is attained in some committees where no rule exists. It is not known whether all Pennsylvania House committees go even as far as is indicated since investigation was confined to a few major ones. In one of the two major committees in the Maryland Senate a record was kept of the dates of committee meetings, the number present at meetings, the numbers of the bills considered and the action taken thereon. No votes were recorded, no notice was included of the appearance of outsiders before the committee, no minute was set down of what transpired save the committee action alone. Conversation with committee chairmen and examination of a few record books indicated that the above record is a rather exceptionally complete one in the Maryland houses. In some committees no official record books at all were used.

The most that can be said regarding committee records as a means of control in the two states is that they are highly uncertain. At best, only a minimum of information is recorded, allowing in no case a determination of individual attitude. At worst, no records of any sort are kept. One Maryland Senator insisted that a careful record of committee proceedings would be highly advisable. Valuable information disclosed at hearings, he continued, is usually lost to the committee members because of delayed action thereafter. If a summary of such information were available for later inspection, the final vote of the committee could be much more intelligent. Whether the legislators would be any more inclined to make such an inspection than they now are to make personal notations on what transpires[3] is, however, quite doubtful.

A careful system of records would, however, tend to give a

[3] Ch. iii, p. 85, above.

certain publicity to what is now in large part a profound secret. " Publicity is perhaps the most essential characteristic of representative government." [4]   Should this in any large measure be true, legislative action being as it is so completely committee action, a record such as that required by the Wisconsin rules [5] would seem highly desirable.

B.   COMMITTEE REPORTS

A second means of committee control is attempted in some state legislatures through certain requirements as to reports.[6] Both chambers in Maryland and Pennsylvania have rules of this character.   The Senate Rules in the former state provide that :

. . . it shall be the duty of said committee to report said Bill or Joint Resolution either favorably or unfavorably with or without amendments.[7]

There follow further formal requirements concerning amended bills.   The House Rule states that :

. . . it shall be the duty of said committee to report said bill or joint resolution either favorably or unfavorably, with or without amendments, or without recommendation.[8]

That this rule is not interpreted as being compulsory is made clear by reference to later tables.[9]   According to statistics there given, Senate committees brought in no report on 10.6 per cent. of all bills referred in the 1927 session, on 12.7 per cent. in 1929.   House committees failed to report 13.1 per cent. of referred bills in the earlier session, 20.0 per cent. in the latter.   Putting the four sessions together, the committees failed to report on approximately 14.2 per cent. of all bills sent to them.   Further examination of the tables cited indi-

---

[4] Quoted from Guizot in L. G. McConachie, Congressional Committees, p. 56.
[5] See page 20, above.
[6] See ch. i, pp. 22-26.
[7] Rule 21, Sec. 5, Rules of the Senate of Maryland, 1929.
[8] Rule 35, Paragraph 4, Rules of the Maryland House of Delegates, 1929.
[9] Tables 14 and 15, ch. v.

cates that the number of "no report" bills is, in nearly every case, larger than that of "unfavorable reports."

There is no Pennsylvania Senate rule as to committee reports except one concerning "negative" reports. Rule 44 provides that:

> . . . A majority of all the members elected to the Senate shall be required to place a negative bill upon the calendar.[10]

The House Rule on the same subject is more explicit, but probably amounts in meaning to about the same thing. It reads:

> . . . The recommendations by a committee that a bill be negatived shall not affect its consideration by the House but the words 'negative recommendation' shall be printed conspicuously on a line above the title of the bill. Such bill shall not be placed upon the calendar except by a majority vote of the members elected to the House, but if such motion be negatived once, it shall not be renewed.
>
> No bill negatived by a committee shall be placed upon the calendar of the House unless a motion to place such bill on the calendar be made within five days after such bill is reported from committee.[11]

Since no example of negative reports was found in the 1929 session, nothing can be said of the application of these rules. There are also rules in both Pennsylvania chambers concerning constitutional provisions prohibiting committee reports on certain designated subjects.[12]

In addition to the above, the Pennsylvania House Rules provide:

> . . . All reports of committees shall be in writing: Provided, that the minority of a committee may make a report in writing, setting forth the reasons for their dissent.[13]

Rule number 39 also describes the procedure in case a committee member assigned to report a bill fails to do so within two days.[14] No case was observed of the use of either of these rules in the 1929 session.

In neither Maryland nor Pennsylvania do the rules make any provision as to the order of committee consideration or report. Casual observation shows, moreover, that there is no

---

[10] Legislative Directory, 1929, p. 23.
[11] Ibid., p. 54, Rule 38.
[12] Ibid., Senate Rule 37, p. 20; House Rule 36, p. 54.
[13] Ibid., House Rule 37, p. 54.   [14] Ibid., pp. 54-55.

apparent relationship between the order of reference and the order of report. In fact, the secretary of one of the important Maryland Senate committees informed the writer that the committee did not act on House bills until the Senate bills were all cleared away.

There is in each Maryland house a further rule concerning what is known as " bequest " bills.

> . . . It shall be the duty of the Committee on the Judiciary, through its chairman, to introduce a House Omnibus Sanction Bequest Bill, which shall take the regular course of bills introduced in the House; and the Judiciary Committee shall not be required to separately report any bill or bills sanctioning any sale, gift, devise or bequest which is included in or covered by the Omnibus Bequest Bill.[15]

With only the changes necessary to make the rule fit the Senate, the rule in the upper house is identical.[16] One of the chief effects of this rule, as it relates to the present study, is that a large number of distinct bills sanctioning bequests are combined by the committees into these Omnibus Bills.

Attention should also be given at this point to the control over conference committees. The only rule found in either Maryland chamber is one providing for the possible election of Senate members of such committees.[17] In 1927, only two conference committee reports were made and in 1929 only four. In none of the 1929 cases did the conference committee present any new material. The amendments proposed by the second house were supported by three of the reports, the original measure by the fourth. No information is available as to whether such committees ever go beyond the points of disagreement.

Attempted control of the Pennsylvania conference committees is to be found in the Joint Rules. It is provided that

> . . . in all cases where a conference takes place, the committee shall be composed of members who vote in the majority on the point or points of difference; but the committee shall not have power or control over any part of a bill, resolution, or order, except such parts upon which a difference exists between the two houses.[18]

---

[15] Rule 36, par. 3, Rules of the Maryland House of Delegates, 1929, p. 15.
[16] Rule 21, Sec. 10, Rules of the Senate of Maryland, 1929, pp. 13-14.
[17] Ibid., Rule 17, p. 9.
[18] Joint Rule 3, Pennsylvania Legislative Directory, 1929, p. 5.

Since this rule was adopted in 1901, it is thought that it might
be considered no longer binding. However, House Rule 33 [19]
provides similarly and would, by controlling the delegation
from one house, control the whole. The 1929 session resulted
in the appointment of eight committees of conference, their
reports being accepted in every case by the chambers.

C. DISCHARGE OF COMMITTEES

There is a rule concerning the discharge of any committee
from further consideration of a bill in each of the four chambers studied. Such rules, as was seen in Chapter I, are rather
prevalent. The Pennsylvania Senate rule, however, seems
designed to protect the committee, rather than to permit its
control.

. . . No committee shall be discharged from the consideration of a
bill within five days of its reference, without unanimous consent of
the Senate.[20]

As to possible Senate action after the five-day guarantee, the
latest ruling discovered was that of the President *pro tempore*
in 1897, holding that a majority of those voting in the Senate
discharges a committee and places the bill on the calendar.[21]
No cases of such discharge seem to have occurred during the
1929 session.

The rule in the House of Representatives reads:

. . . That when a bill or resolution has been ten days in the hands
of a committee after having been referred to it any committee may
be discharged from the further consideration of the bill or resolution
by a majority vote of all the members elect.[22]

The rule as thus stated was passed in the session of 1925. It
superseded a rule of long standing which permitted discharge
upon the vote of sixty members. Frequent use seems to have
been made of the old rule—in fact the frequency of its use
brought its repeal. It was felt to be a waste of time to bring
measures back to the House only to have them defeated for

---

[19] Ibid., p. 53.
[20] Rule 42, Senate Rules, ibid., p. 23.
[21] The Pennsylvania Manual, 1929, p. 985.
[22] Rule 40, House Rules, Pennsylvania Legislative Directory, p. 55.

want of a constitutional majority. Accordingly the rule was changed to its present form. Since then only one attempt has been made to recover a bill.[23] On April 8, 1929, a motion to recall House Bill No. 742 was made. The vote was twenty-six affirmative to one hundred fifty-two negative. While the rule in its present form may save a certain amount of time, it undeniably enhances the power of the committees. Furthermore, the former chance for publicity on a debatable matter is gone. Is sufficient time gained to offset the possible advantages of an easier discharge system? The majority floor leader expressed it as his opinion that the rule in its present form allowed sufficient control. The assistant director of the Legislative Reference Bureau writes:

. . . We personally believe it was a good change, and saves much time without unnecessarily throttling legislation.[24]

However, a resolution was introduced on April 18, 1929, suggesting among other things the advisability of a rule making reports of all bills mandatory. The spirit of the Pennsylvania House Rule is in general agreement with that of the national House of Representatives where the discharge of a committee from further consideration of a bill now requires a petition signed by a majority of the members.[25] In the United States Senate, however, " it is always possible for the majority to discharge a committee " after one days' notice.[26]

In contrast to the difficult procedure necessary to recall a bill from committee in the Pennsylvania chambers, the discharge rules in Maryland are comparatively easy of applica-

---

[23] Information regarding the change of rule was obtained by letter from the Legislative Reference Bureau at Harrisburg.
[24] Letter dated March 11, 1930, to Philip Sterling, majority floor leader.
[25] Rule XXVII, 4, Rules of the House of Representatives. Until recent times such discharge could only be accomplished by " suspension of the rules or on a report from the Committee on Rules." A. C. Hinds' Precedents of the House of Representatives, IV, 360, sec. 3533. A discharge rule, however, was adopted in 1910 and amended in 1912. A later form, allowing discharge upon a petition signed by 150 members, dates from 1924. The present rule is of December 7, 1925. During the short session of the Seventy-First Congress the existing rule has been bitterly assailed.
[26] Hinds' Precedents, IV, 981, note 2.

tion. The two houses have rules almost identical in form.
The rule, applicable generally in the House of Delegates,
provides that

> . . . Each bill or joint resolution (except the Budget Bill or any
> other hereinafter specifically provided for) referred to a committee
> of the House during the first thirty days of the session shall be
> reported by the committee to which referred not later than twenty
> days after its reference to said committee; and those referred to
> a committee of the House after the first thirty days of the session
> shall be reported by the committee to which they were referred not
> later than fifteen days from the date of their reference; provided,
> however, that upon the failure of any committee to report a bill or
> joint resolution referred to it within the time herein specified with
> respect thereto, any fifteen members may present a demand in
> writing for the return to the House of such bill or joint resolution
> from the committee to which it has been referred, which demand
> may be made at any time in the order of business designated as
> 'Reports of Standing Committees,' or 'Reports of Select Commit-
> tees,' according to [as?] the bill or joint resolution may have been
> referred to a standing or select committee, and such demand shall
> be entered in the Journal, and shall constitute the demand of the
> House, and said bill or joint resolution shall thereupon take the
> same place as though it had been reported by said committee without
> recommendation.[27]

The Senate rule is identical in wording save for the substi-
tution of the word " Senate " for " House " and of " three
senators " for " fifteen members," the omission of the last two
words " without recommendation " and the addition at the
close of the following:

> . . . unless, upon the request of the Chairman, or Acting Chairman,
> of such Committee for further time for the consideration by the
> Committee of such Bill or Joint Resolution, the Senate shall, by a
> majority vote, grant said Committee additional time in which to
> consider such Bill or Resolution. Such demand shall not be con-
> strued as a reflection upon or a discourtesy to any such Committee.[28]

What do these rules signify? Put briefly, they provide
a means, supposedly, whereby a small number of legislators
can compel a committee to report a measure after the expiration of a certain period of time. They do not, as a casual
reading might suggest, make a report of all bills compulsory.
In fact, of all bills referred in the 1929 session, approximately

---

[27] Rule 35, par. 6, Rules of the Maryland House of Delegates, 1929,
pp. 14-15.

[28] Rule 21, Sec. 8, Rules of the Senate of Maryland, 1929, pp. 12-13.

16 per cent. were never reported at all.[29]   Of one hundred twenty-three House Bills introduced during the first thirty days of the session in 1929, only thirty-five were returned during the twenty-day period specified by the rule.   The Senate referred one hundred four bills during the same period, only twenty-nine of which were reported within twenty days.   There were 483 House Bills referred to House committees after the first thirty days, of which 270 were reported within the fifteen-day period, 87 after a longer time and 126 not at all.   In the Senate, committee reports on 349 Senate bills, introduced after the first thirty days, were distributed as follows: within the fifteen-day period, 231; after the fifteen-day period, 65; no reports, 53.   The rules do not, evidently, require the return of referred measures save upon the written demand of the prescribed number of legislators.   Yet even here, there are limits to such action, expressed, interpreted, or understood.

The first limit demanding attention is the period of time specified.   Bills referred to a committee during the first thirty days of the session are subject to the rule after twenty days. Later bills may be recalled after fifteen days.   What effect will the prevalent late introduction of bills have in the application of the rule?   If only five days be allowed for second house action, all bills introduced during the last twenty days of the session will be beyond the application of the rule.   During the 1929 session, 89 Senate Bills out of a total of 453 introduced, and 150 House Bills out of a total of 606 introduced, were thus practically beyond any effect of the rule.   In percentages, 22.5 per cent. of all bills introduced in the two chambers were thus for practical purposes incapable of being affected by the rule in the house of origin.   Note, however, the limit placed upon the rule when the measures reach the second house.   Out of 311 Senate Bills which reached the House in 1929, 188 or 60.5 per cent. of them were referred to House committees during the last fifteen days of the session.   In the Senate, 214 House Bills out of 370 referred to Senate committees, or about 57.8 per cent., reached these committees too

---

[29] See Table 15, ch. v.

late for any possible application of the rule. Such percentages are based, too, upon the bare fifteen-day limit. If time be added for the passage of bills by the chamber without suspension of the rules, for a certain amount of deliberation and perhaps amendment, making necessary re-submission to the house of origin, many more bills would be exempted from the rule.

It was unofficially reported to the author that an interpretation was placed upon the Senate rule in the 1929 session which would still farther limit its application. According to this report—confirmation is lacking—the time limit of fifteen days, or twenty early in the session, is to extend from the date on which the committee actually comes into possession of the bill. The rule specifies " date of reference " but, conceivably, several days might elapse between that and actual committee receipt. The General Assembly usually adjourns on Wednesday or Thursday until Monday of the following week. Bills referred during the last legislative day of the week would not therefore be subject to the provisions of the discharge rule until fifteen days after the following Monday, that is an actual period of perhaps twenty days instead of fifteen. Should such an interpretation be adhered to, it might possibly have serious effects upon the workability of the rule. A committee chairman might in his discretion fail to secure the referred bill from the office of the Secretary until such a time as to prevent its forced return to the Senate. Such a misapplication of the rule would be particularly possible during the latter part of the session and might remove almost all measures in the second house from its contemplated control. Another interpretation in the Senate, not officially reported, serves to weaken its control of the committees. The chair made a ruling that the fifteen-day provision was intended to guarantee the committee that length of time for consideration. To recall a bill before the expiration of that time, it was held, would require a suspension of the rule, necessitating a two-thirds vote. Such an interpretation was without doubt never intended and no justification for it is evident. The discharge rule applies only to bills retained more than the specified

7

time. The Senate's control over measures within that time
remains what it always was. By generally recognized rules of
parliamentary procedure,[30] a majority vote, or at most a
majority of the total membership, would suffice to recall the
measure. Not being recorded, the interpretation is not apt,
however, to be considered a precedent.

There seems still further to be a general understanding that
the rule will not be invoked frequently. Committee chairmen
do not seem to relish the idea of its application. Rather than
submit to it, they will bring in an unfavorable report in
response to a threat of petition. Among the membership of
the chambers, too, leniency toward the committee seems prevalent. This attitude was noted particularly in connection
with a measure forced out of committee in the House of
Delegates in the last session. The committee, in response to
the author's request for action, had asked for more time.
That request had been denied and the petition presented. On
the floor of the House, delegates spoke and voted against the
measure, as they explained, in protest against such practice.

In spite of the above limitations, however, the rule seems
to have certain value. Measurement of its application or
success is of course impossible. In the first place there is no
method of determining how effective it is as a threat. No
doubt exists that in many cases the knowledge that it is about
to be applied is sufficient to bring committee action. The
committee may feel that an unfavorable report will be more
effective in disposing of the measure than a forced return
which puts the bill before the house as " without recommendation." The chairman of the Ways and Means committee cited
an instance of the threatened use of the rule in connection
with a bill in his committee. To forestall the filing of the
petition, the committee reported " unfavorably," following
that with a motion to recommit which prevailed by a vote of
fifty-seven to forty-three.

The actual use of the discharge rule in any one session can

[30] Henry M. Robert, Parliamentary Law, p. 109, The Century Com-
pany, 1923.

of course presumably be determined. Two petitions were put
into operation in the 1929 session, so far as the records show.
One measure so recalled was indefinitely postponed, nine of
the original eighteen signers voting for that action. The total
vote stood at eighty-two for postponement to nineteen against.
A second bill was brought in on the last day of the session
only to be recommitted to another committee upon motion of
the chairman of the first without a recorded vote. The
Senate Journal reveals no instance of the application of the
rule. Apparently then the value is potential rather than applied. Like the initiative or the recall, it is the gun behind
the door.

Conversations with members of the House and Senate disclosed a rather general satisfaction with the rule. Its value
as a threat was emphasized by many. The chairman of an
important House committee against whom use of the rule
had been threatened admitted its justice, saying, " Every
member has a right to make a fight for his own bill." A few
members considered the rule not stringent enough, too many
bills escaping its possible application.[31]

---

[31] For comments on committee control in other States, see Patton,
pp. 222-225; Walter Thompson, " Our Legislative Mills: Wisconsin " in National Municipal Review, XII, 602-603; Hanford, pp. 42-
43; Dodds, ch. iv; and Ralph S. Boots, " Our Legislative Mills:
Nebraska," in National Municipal Review, XIII, 113-114.

CHAPTER V

WORK OF COMMITTEES IN MARYLAND AND PENNSYLVANIA

A. LEGISLATIVE BILL HISTORY

Having seen how legislative committees are organized, under what procedure they work, and how their actions are controlled by their superior bodies, it remains now to consider the work which they perform. No attention is paid here to committee work in the confirmation of appointments or the supervision of state institutions or administrative agencies, nor to that of such formal committees as those on Printing, Printed Bills, and Supervision of Employees. Instead, consideration is here given to their more substantive legislative work. Tables 14, 15, and 16 are an attempt to summarize statistically some of the facts of legislative bill history in the sessions studied which seem to have direct relation to the committee system. These tables cover both Senate and House bills, showing action thereon in both houses, both the total number of bills and the percentage being shown in connection with each different action recorded. The classification of bills in items number I and II is more or less arbitrary. In the former, the periods are each approximately one-third of the length of the session save that the last five days of the third period are tabulated separately as a fourth. In the latter,

TABLE 14.* BILL HISTORY IN MARYLAND GENERAL ASSEMBLY—1927.

| | SENATE BILLS | | | | HOUSE BILLS | | | |
| | In Senate | | In House | | In House | | In Senate | |
	No.	Per Cent.	No.	Per Cent.	No.	Per Cent.	No.	Per Cent.
I. *Date of Reference to Committee*								
Jan. 11–Feb. 4..	124	25.3	7	1.9	202	28.7	0	0.0
Feb. 5–Mar. 6..	194	34.6	85	22.5	219	31.1	95	20.0
Mar. 7–Mar. 28.	170	39.5	153	40.6	281	40.0	222	46.6
Mar. 29–April 4	3	0.6	132	35.0	1	0.1	159	33.4
Total.........	491	100.0	377	100.0	703	99.9	476	100.0

| | SENATE BILLS | | | | HOUSE BILLS | | | |
| | In Senate | | In House | | In Senate | | In House | |
	No.	Per Cent.	No.	Per Cent.	No.	Per Cent.	No.	Per Cent.
II. *Calendar Days Elapsing Before Date of Report*								
0– 5	105	23.9	223	63.5	161	27.4	272	63.5
6–15	173	39.7	83	23.6	226	38.5	114	26.6
16–30	104	23.9	32	9.1	85	14.5	37	8.6
31–45	33	7.6	9	2.6	44	7.5	5	1.2
46–60	7	1.6	4	1.1	30	5.1	0	0.0
61–75	13	3.0	0	0.0	41	7.0	0	0.0
76–90	2	0.5	0	0.0	0	0.0	0	0.0
Total........	436	100.2	351	99.9	587	100.0	428	99.9
II. *Nature of Committee Report*								
None	55	11.2	26	6.9	116	16.5	48	10.1
Favorable	295	60.1	282	74.8	423	60.2	322	67.6
Unfavorable ...	53	10.8	24	6.3	73	10.4	39	8.2
Fav. with amend.	80	16.3	45	11.9	77	11.0	63	13.3
No recommend..	8	1.6	0	0.0	14	2.0	4	0.8
Total........	491	100.0	377	99.9	703	100.1	476	100.0
V. *Action Taken on Report*								
Accepted	395	90.6	329	93.7	517	88.1	401	93.7
Amended	3	0.7	1	0.3	7	1.2	11	2.5
Recommitted ..	36	8.3	5	1.4	56	9.5	11	2.5
Rejected	2	0.5	4	1.1	8	1.4	5	1.2
No action......	0	0.0	12 [1]	3.4	0	0.0	0	0.0
Total........	436	100.1	351	99.9	588	100.2	428	99.9
V. *Nature of Report on Recommitted Bills*								
None	4		0		21		3	
Favorable	13		1		17		3	
Unfavorable ...	4		1		4		2	
Fav. with amend.	14		3		13		3	
No recommend..	1		0		1		0	
Total........	36		5		56		11	
VI. *Action Taken on Second Report*								
Accepted	28		4		31		8	
Amended	1		0		0		0	
Recommitted ..	2 [2]		0		3 [3]		0	
Rejected	1		0		0		0	
No action......	0		1 [4]		1		0	
Total........	32		5		35		8	
II. *Action Taken on Amendments of Second House*								
Concurred	48				68			
Rejected	1				3			
Conference report adopted..	1				1			

[1] All unfavorable reports.
[2] No report on one; favorable report, accepted, on the other.
[3] No report on any.   [4] Unfavorable report.

TABLE 15.*   BILL HISTORY IN MARYLAND GENERAL ASSEMBLY—1929.

| | SENATE BILLS | | | | HOUSE BILLS | | | |
| | In Senate | | In House | | In House | | In Senate | |
	No.	Per Cent.	No.	Per Cent.	No.	Per Cent.	No.	Per Cent.
I. *Date of Reference to Committee*								
Jan. 4–31......	104	22.9	4	1.3	123	20.3	1	0.3
Feb. 1–Mar. 2..	159	35.2	72	23.2	208	34.4	82	22.2
Mar. 3–25......	187	41.2	146	47.0	275	45.4	200	54.1
Mar. 26–April 1	3	0.7	89	28.6	0	0.0	87	23.5
Total........	453	100.0	311	100.1	606	100.1	370	100.1
II. *Calendar Days Elapsing Before Date of Report*								
0– 5	64	17.1	187	67.7	130	29.8	190	55.2
6–15	195	52.0	58	21.0	168	38.4	105	30.5
16–30	69	18.4	21	7.6	105	24.0	37	10.8
31–45	24	6.4	8	2.9	19	4.3	9	2.6
46–60	19	5.1	2	0.7	14	3.0	3	0.9
61–75	4	1.1	0	0.0	1	0.2	0	0.0
Total........	375	100.1	276	99.9	437	99.7	344	100.0
III. *Nature of Committee Report*								
None	78	17.4	35	11.3	169	27.9	26	7.0
Favorable	251	55.5	237	76.2	311	51.3	273	73.8
Unfavorable ...	63	13.7	8	2.6	46	7.6	29	7.8
Fav. with amend.	56	12.3	31	10.0	70	11.6	40	10.8
No recommend..	5	1.1	0	0.0	10	1.6	2	0.5
Total........	453	100.0	311	100.1	606	100.1	370	99.9
IV. *Action Taken on Report*								
Accepted	324	85.9	258	92.1	388	88.8	321	91.5
Amended	17	4.5	8	2.9	8	1.8	13	3.7
Recommitted ..	30	8.0	13	4.6	38	8.7	13	3.7
Rejected	5	1.3	1	0.4	3	0.7	4	1.1
No action......	1	0.3	0	0.0	0	0.0	0	0.0
Total........	377	100.0	280	100.0	437	100.0	351	100.0
V. *Nature of Report on Recommitted Bills*								
None	4		2		13		2	
Favorable	13		5		14		10	
Unfavorable ...	4		0		2		1	
Fav. with amend.	9		6		9		0	
Total........	30		13		38		13	

	SENATE BILLS				HOUSE BILLS			
	In Senate		In House		In House		In Senate	
	No.	Per Cent.	No.	Per Cent.	No.	Per Cent.	No.	Per Cent.
VI. *Action Taken on Second Report*								
Accepted	19	10			22	10		
Amended	5	0			1	0		
Recommitted ...	2 [1]		1 [2]		1 [3]		1 [4]	
Rejected	0	0			1	0		
Total........	26	11			25	11		
VII. *Action Taken on Amendments of Second House*								
Concurred	39				48			
Rejected	0				1			
Conference report adopted..	1				3 [5]			

[1] No report on one; favorable with amendments, accepted, on the other.
[2] Favorable report, accepted.
[3] Favorable with amendments, report accepted, bill lost.
[4] Favorable report, accepted.
[5] Senate amendment accepted on two, rejected on the third.

TABLE 16.* BILL HISTORY IN PENNSYLVANIA GENERAL ASSEMBLY—1929.

	SENATE BILLS				HOUSE BILLS			
	In Senate		In House		In House		In Senate	
	No.	Per Cent.	No.	Per Cent.	No.	Per Cent.	No.	Per Cent.
I. *Date of Reference to Committee*								
Jan. 1–Feb. 5...	413	44.2	12	2.3	829	43.3	1	0.1
Feb. 6–Mar. 13..	357	38.2	134	26.2	767	40.1	229	26.9
Mar. 14–April 13	164	17.5	330	64.5	317	16.6	600	70.6
April 14–April 18	1	0.1	36	7.0	0	0.0	20	2.4
Total........	935	100.0	512	100.0	1913	100.0	850	100.0
II. *Calendar Days Elapsing Before Date of Report*								
0– 5	120	21.5	234	51.4	78	7.7	428	55.5
6–15	194	34.7	168	36.9	456	45.1	270	35.0
16–30	91	16.3	35	7.7	190	18.8	56	7.3
31–45	53	9.5	12	2.6	129	12.8	11	1.4
46–60	41	7.3	4	0.9	93	9.2	3	0.4
61–75	52	9.3	2	0.4	60	5.9	3	0.4
76–90	8	1.5	0	0.0	4	0.4	0	0.0
Total........	559	100.1	455	99.9	1010	99.9	771	100.0
III. *Nature of Committee Report*								
None	376	40.2	57	11.1	903	47.2	79	9.3
As committed..	367	39.3	394	77.0	687	35.9	666	78.4
As amended....	191	20.4	61	11.9	271	14.2	105	12.4
No recommend..	1	0.1	0	0.0	52	2.7	0	0.0
Total........	935	100.0	512	100.0	1913	100.0	850	100.1

| | SENATE BILLS | | | | HOUSE BILLS | | | |
| | In Senate | | In House | | In House | | In Senate | |
	No.	Per Cent.	No.	Per Cent.	No.	Per Cent.	No.	Per Cent.
IV. *Action Taken on Report*								
Accepted	412	72.4	379	82.4	621	61.5	653	84.7
Amended	75	13.2	53	11.5	154	15.2	55	7.1
Recommitted ...	78	13.7	24	5.2	139	13.8	60	7.9
Rejected	2	0.3	2	0.4	10	1.0	0	0.0
Dropped	1	0.2	2	0.4	34	3.4	3	0.4
Re-referred	1	0.2	0	0.0	52	5.1	0	0.0
Total........	569	100.0	460	99.9	1010	100.0	771	100.1
V. *Nature of Report on Recommitted Bills*								
None	38		7		103		24	
As committed..	15		12		55		15	
As amended....	26		5		31		21	
No recommend..	0		0		2		0	
Total........	79		24		191		60	
VI. *Action Taken on Second Report*								
Accepted	29		12		62		32	
Amended	3		1		9		4	
Recommitted ..	9 [1]		3 [2]		11 [3]		1 [4]	
Rejected	1		0		6		0	
Dropped	0		1		0		0	
Total........	42		17		88		37	
VII. *Action Taken on Amendments of Second House*								
Concurred......	90				148			
No concurrence necessary.....	..				1			
Conference report adopted..	3				5			
VIII. *Measures Recalled from the Governor*								
Amended and returned.......	20				27			
Returned as recalled........	6				1			
Tabled	2				8			
Recommitted ...	1 (no report)				0			
Recall refused..	0				1			
Total........	29				37 [5]			

[1] No report on five; two each "as committed" and "as amended"; Senate accepted two, amended two.

[2] No report on two; "as committed," accepted, on one.

[3] No report on seven; two each "as committed" and "as amended"; House accepted three, amended one.

[4] No report.   [5] Two measures recalled twice.

* The information contained in these three tables has been compiled from the following sources:

For Maryland—Journal of Proceedings of the Senate, 1927 and 1929 sessions; Journal of Proceedings of the House of Delegates, 1927 and 1929 sessions; Card index history of Senate and House Bills in office of the Department of Legislative Reference, Baltimore, for 1927 and 1929 sessions;

For Pennsylvania—History of Senate Bills, session of 1929; History of House Bills, session of 1929; Legislative Journal, session of 1929.

the periods are generally fifteen calendar days save for the first two. Here it seemed desirable to tabulate committee activity in smaller units so as to indicate more accurately the bills remaining in committee for only a brief period. Since in the Pennsylvania legislature the committees, with rare exceptions, do not report negatively on bills, the Pennsylvania table omits that item in sections III and V. Section VIII is added to Table 16 since the prevalent practice in Pennsylvania of recalling bills from the governor would seem to be not entirely dissociated from committee action.

1. Date of Reference to Committees.

Examination of this section on the three tables reveals some interesting information. It will be noted first that the 1927 and 1929 sessions of the Maryland General Assembly are, on a percentage basis, strikingly similar. In both the house of origin and the second house, the share of bills received by the committees in each calendar period is comparatively equal. The largest differences are to be seen in the cases of reference of House bills in the House during the first calendar period and of Senate and House bills to committees of the second house during the last five days of the session. But despite these differences, the highest percentage rate in every case is to be found in the shortened third period and the lowest (among the three major periods) is in the first. The congestion toward the end of the session is evident. Committees of the second house receive from 75 to 80 per cent. of all the bills sent over from the house of origin during the last third of the session. In addition they receive from 40 to 45.4 per cent. of all bills in their own house during this period. And, besides both these classes of bills, the committees still have in their possession an unknown quantity of bills referred to them in earlier periods and not yet disposed of. It is noticed that from 23.5 to 35 per cent. of all bills coming from the house of origin are referred to committees of the second house during the last five days of the session. When this tendency toward late session reference is combined with the prevalent concentration of measures in two major committees in each house,[1] the overburdening becomes extreme, with necessary curtailment of committee consideration.

A contrast to the above is presented in the Pennsylvania table. The number of bills sent to committee during the last five days of the session is negligible when compared to the Maryland practice. On the other hand, the largest reference percentage in the house of origin is found in the first calendar period instead of the third. It is true that the third period includes a higher percentage rate for references in the second house than was found in Maryland—65 per cent. to 70 per cent. instead of 40 per cent. to 54 per cent.—but the small rate found in the fourth period more than offsets the larger one in the third. Further, the wider distribution of bills among committees in Pennsylvania tends to leave the committees much less overburdened near the close of the session than in Maryland.

2. Calendar Days Elapsing before Date of Report.

The data under this heading needs a word of explanation. Information being unavailable as to when the committee actually came into possession of a bill, the only measuring-stick to use was that of elapsed time between date of reference and date of report. Since during that period the bill must often have to be printed or reprinted, the actual committee possession of the bill is somewhat shorter. This fact is of particular importance in the first group, where the maximum elapsed time is five days. The fourth and eighth columns in all three tables show that over 50 per cent. of all measures reported from committees in the second house were in committee a maximum of five days. It should be noted too that the elapsed time is based on calendar days and not on legislative days. In cases where bills are referred late in the week, the five-day period may be barely the next legislative day so that the bill may be actually in committee possession for only one day.

---

[1] See Table 5, ch. ii.

That the committees themselves contribute somewhat to the end-of-the-session rush is evidenced by the number of bills retained in committee for an extended period. The committees in the houses of origin in the three sessions tabulated kept bills for a period upward of a month in percentages varying from 7.5 in the Maryland House in 1929 to 28.3 in the Pennsylvania House of 1929. These percentages do not, of course, include bills unreported, which, in the case of Pennsylvania, amount to almost half of all bills referred.

A decided contrast is noted in the elapsed time when percentages in the house of origin are set beside those in the second house. In the five-day period, the two Maryland tables show for the houses of origin a variation of from 17.1 to 29.8 per cent., while in the second houses the percentages run from 55.2 to 67.7. This shows roughly a comparative ratio of 2.5. The same comparison, drawn from the Pennsylvania table, shows 21.5 per cent. as compared to 51.4 per cent. in the Senate and 7.7 per cent. as compared to 55.5 per cent. in the House. A similar contrast is evident in the case of bills retained over thirty days. The Maryland tables again show a variation of from 7.5 to 19.6 per cent. in the houses of origin as compared to one from 1.2 to 3.7 [2] per cent. in the second houses, or a rough comparative ratio of 4.4. The Pennsylvania contrast in the same matter is 26.6 per cent. to 3.9 per cent. in the Senate, 26.3 per cent. to 2.2 per cent. in the House. Generally speaking, the committees in the houses of origin retain bills in their possession for a much longer period than those in the second houses, whether or not this means more careful consideration.

As to the absolute period of committee retention of bills it is noticeable that in every case, as evidenced in the three tables, the highest percentage of bills for any period is found in the 6-15 day group for the houses of origin, in the 0-5 day group for second houses. No attempt is made to strike

---

[2] These four percentages are in each case the sum of the three or four items given in the tables for periods longer than thirty days. Only the minimum and maximum for the two sessions are put into the text.

an average for the length of time in committee, but the median for reported bills would lie in every case in the latter part of the 6-15 day period for the houses of origin and in the latter part of the 0-5 day period for the second houses. The entire comparison reveals a decided slowness of action in the case of a considerable percentage of all bills in the houses of origin and a remarkable speed in the second houses due undoubtedly in many cases to the necessity caused by the lateness of their receipt of bills. Obviously, if nearly half of all bills are first introduced in the last thirty days of the session, printed and given average consideration by the committee of the house of origin, but little time will remain for second house action.

3.   Nature of Committee Report.

This section of the tables reveals first of all the importance of committees as sifting agencies. In the Maryland houses of origin the percentage of bills not reported from committee at all varies from 11.2 to 28.1, or a rough average of 18.3 per cent. In Pennsylvania the percentages are 40.2 for the Senate and 47.2 for the House. In the second houses the Maryland tables reveal a variation of from 6.9 to 11.3 per cent., or a rough average of 8.8 per cent. The Pennsylvania percentages for the same item are 11.1 and 9.3. Committees in the houses of origin, it is to be noted, kill from two to four times as many bills compared to the total number received as do the second houses. The contrast shown above as between Maryland and Pennsylvania is, however, inaccurate. No bills in the latter case were reported unfavorably. If the " un-favorable report " percentages in the Maryland tables, most of which reports are accepted without question by the houses, are added to the " no-report " percentages, a total of from 22.0 to 35.7 per cent. results to compare with the 40.2 to 47.2 per cent. of Pennsylvania. In the second houses a like combination produces from 13.2 per cent. to 18.3 in Maryland compared to 9.3 and 11.1 per cent. in Penn-sylvania. In brief, the committees in the Pennsylvania houses of origin kill a considerably larger percentage of all bills received than is true in Maryland. In the second houses the comparative percentages are reversed. Roughly, the committees in the Pennsylvania houses of origin kill a half more bills than those in Maryland, while in the latter state the second house committees kill a half more than in the former.

The next item concerns "favorable" or "as committed" reports. These are measures approved without change by the committees. In Maryland the houses of origin receive back from their committees from 51.3 to 60.2 per cent. of all bills referred,—an approximate average of 56.83 per cent.— with a favorable report attached. Little distinction is to be seen between Senate and House committees. The Pennsylvania percentages are considerably lower—39.3 per cent. for the Senate and 35.9 per cent. for the House. The explanation is partly found in the higher number of bills killed in committee, partly, as appears later, in the greater tendency of Pennsylvania committees to amend. In all cases the second houses receive back a larger percentage of referred bills from their committees with favorable reports than do the houses of origin. The Maryland percentages vary from 67.6 to 76.2, showing an approximate average of 73.1 per cent. The Pennsylvania second house committee reports of a favorable nature are 77 per cent. for the Senate, 78.4 per cent. for the House. It is noteworthy that the Pennsylvania committees in each house approve without change nearly the same percentage of the bills coming from the other house and that such approval is given approximately twice as often as is true when committees of the houses of origin are considering the measures. These higher percentages in the second houses of both states is partially explained by the smaller number of bills killed as well as by the generally lower amendment rate.

The extent to which "favorable" reports are returned deserves emphasis. A comparison of the number of such reports with the number of all others—unfavorable, with amendments and without recommendation—reveals a preponderant tendency toward reporting bills without change. In the houses of origin in both states, approximately two-thirds of all reports from committee are of this nature. In the second houses in Maryland 80 per cent. of all reports are "favorable" while in Pennsylvania the reports "as committed" amount to 86 per cent. of all second house committee returns. Thus is indicated in both states a considerably greater tendency in the second houses than in those of origin toward "favorable" committee action.

The "unfavorable" reports, although unknown in the 1929 session of the Pennsylvania legislature, are of considerable importance in Maryland. Generally there are more of such reports in the house of origin than in the second house. Examination of individual cases reveals that a good many such reports are the result of pressure applied to the committee. In certain cases, acceptance of the committee report being assured, the unfavorable report was brought in to show the overwhelming opposition to the bill or to relieve the committee of the responsibility of killing it. Occasionally, as seen above,[3] such reports are the result of the use of the discharge rule. On a comparative basis, Senate committees seem to be more inclined to report House bills unfavorably than House committees are Senate bills. Since unfavorable reports are usually accepted, this item should be considered in connection with that of "no report," two lines above in the tables. A combination of these two items shows markedly the importance of the "sifting" process, particularly in committees of the houses of origin. The 1929 table (No. 15) discloses that, of the Senate bills, 31.1 per cent. were started toward ultimate oblivion by Senate committees, 13.9 per cent. by the House committees. Of the House bills, 35.7 per cent. were so treated by committees of the House and only 14.8 per cent. by Senate committees.

Despite the large number of favorable reports noted in the paragraph preceding the last, the committees do turn back to their houses a considerable number of amended bills. The extent of this is indicated in the fourth line of section III of the tables (third line in the Pennsylvania Table). Com-

---

[3] Ch. iv.

mittees of the houses of origin report with amendments an approximate average of 15 per cent. of all bills referred in the Maryland General Assembly, 17 per cent. in Pennsylvania. Second house committee averages in the same order are approximately 11.5 and 12. An analysis of all amendments made in the 1929 Maryland session shows the following as to their nature. Amendments are classified as " Technical " if they are for merely formal rather than substantive purposes. For instance, corrections in spelling, names, punctuation and grammatical construction are designated " Technical." Changes in the provisions of a bill, whether great or small, are listed as " Content."

TABLE 17. NATURE OF AMENDMENTS, 1929 MARYLAND GENERAL ASSEMBLY.

| | SENATE BILLS | | HOUSE BILLS | |
	In Senate	In House	In House	In Senate
Amendments, Technical...	5	4	12	11
Amendments, Content	75	38	71 [1]	42 [2]
Amendments, Total	80	42	83	53

[1] One amendment (by the committee) was a substitute for the bill referred, and treated of an entirely different matter.
[2] A similar situation appeared here, but, after acceptance of the report by the Senate, the bill was recommitted and the amendment withdrawn.

That the number of " technical " amendments is so low may be largely due to the activities of a very efficient legislative reference and bill-drafting bureau. The " content " amendments vary, of course, from those of very minor import to those which leave but little of the original intent of the bill. A grouping of them, however, on grounds of importance is entirely impossible. Neither was it found practicable to study the matter of re-writing bills. To some extent individual bills are re-written in committee, sometimes without much change in idea, sometimes to combine features of different bills. Where two or more measures are combined into one by mere process of committee amendment, the statistics show only the report of a bill as amended and the death of any others combined with it. The extent of such practice, however, seemed comparatively slight and, in any case, quite immeasurable. Here it need only be noted that the amending process, judged solely by the number of bills affected, is of considerable importance.

The "no recommendation" item is of comparative insignificance save as it has relation to the process of reference of bills. Nearly all bills listed under this heading were returned to the house for reference to what seemed to be more appropriate committees than those first receiving them. This matter was discussed in a former chapter.[4]

4. Action Taken on Report.

It is in Section IV of these tables that the real importance of legislative committees becomes evident. The houses of origin in Maryland accept outright the reports of their committees in approximately 88 per cent. of the cases. Second houses accept without change in 92.7 per cent. of all cases. Pennsylvania houses of origin accept approximately 67 per cent. of all reports (72.4 per cent. for the Senate, 61.5 per cent. for the House). Second house acceptance amounts to approximately 83.5 per cent. These percentages, however, are not as high as the real facts of the case show. In reality all of the "no-report" bills should be included in any computation of the extent of acceptance of committee action. If these are included, the base for computing percentages must then be the number of bills referred rather than the number reported. The percentages of acceptance then become 90.6 for the Maryland houses of origin and 94.1 for the second houses. For Pennsylvania, likewise, the percentages change to 81.2 and 85.7. Such percentages indicate that the committees are much more than advisory bodies, their action being final in most cases.

Other factors, however, even within the field of reported bills, affect the "acceptance" figures. The "no action" item, for instance, in the Maryland tables included in one case a bill reported by the committee without recommenda-

---

[4] Ch. iii.

tion. The twelve bills so tabulated in the 1927 session had all been reported unfavorably. " No action " therefore meant acceptance. The " dropped " item in the Pennsylvania table is not exactly comparable because all bills so treated had been reported " as committed " or " as amended." However, examination of individual cases discloses that most of them certainly were dropped at the request of the committee or with its consent. Such action might occur where some other measure covered the same field or where for some other reason no one cared to push the measure along.

In addition to these items, the " recommitted " group needs consideration in connection with " accepted " reports. It might be supposed that, by recommitting a bill, the house was demanding further consideration by the committee. In most cases that does not seem to be the case. Instead, the committee itself usually asks for recommitment. Numerous instances of committee action were observed in which there was an understanding in committee that recommitment would be requested. Committee members, charged with the duty of presenting the committee report, were often enjoined to bring the measure back to committee before final action took place in the house. To be sure, in certain cases, the chamber sought further consideration by recommitment either to the same or a new committee, but generally such action is at the committee's request. Such being the case, the percentages listed under this item would in large part be added to the " accepted " group, thus raising that percentage a considerable amount.

The two items remaining—" amended " and " rejected "— appear on the surface to indicate action by the chamber contrary to or by way of change of the committee report. Even the " rejected " reports, however, may be misleading. For instance, in the 1929 Maryland table, the following facts regarding " rejected " reports appear upon examination. All of them had been " unfavorable " from committee. Of the three House committee " rejected " reports of House Bills one failed finally to pass the House, one was amended, and only one was a complete reversal of the committee action. Of

8

the four Senate committee reports on House bills " rejected " by the Senate, one was amended so as to be innocuous, one was amended and later requested back from the House, and two were complete reversals of committee action. Of the five Senate bill " unfavorable " reports " rejected " by the Senate, one was later recommitted and died in committee, the other four being real rejections. The House " tabled " one " favorable " committee report on a Senate bill. The reports of Pennsylvania committees on Senate bills " rejected " by Senate and House—two in each—are really " rejected " reports. Of the ten " rejected " reports on House bills by the House, five show so small a vote in favor of accepting the report on the question of final passage as to raise grave doubts as to the real position of the committee thereon. The other five seem to be real rejections.

The extent to which the houses amend the measures as reported from committees is indicated in the second line of this section. It is to be noticed that the percentages are consistently small in the Maryland tables, the highest of any for the two sessions being 4.5 per cent. Curiously, the Senate, when acting upon House bills, amended approximately twice as many measures as the House itself had done. The House, on the contrary, amended only slightly more than half as many Senate bills as the Senate did. The Pennsylvania percentages are much higher, showing a rough average of 14.2 per cent. in the houses of origin and of 9.2 per cent. in the second houses.[5] In this item again, however, the table statistics do not reveal the entire situation. An examination of the amendments made from the floor and accepted by the chambers indicates that even here the committee attitude is the controlling one. Using the 1929 Maryland session as an illustration, a careful check was made of the source of such amendments. In the Senate, amendments were offered from the floor and accepted in the case of twenty bills. Some bills

---

[5] Since the " unfavorable " reports are included in the base for the Maryland percentages and not for Pennsylvania, the comparison is not accurate. The 4.5 per cent. becomes 5.4 per cent. if the " unfavorable " reports are excluded from consideration.

were thus amended twice. The committee, or members thereof, offered thirteen amendments, the authors seven, and seven were proposed by other senators. In only one case was there significant committee opposition to such amendments and even then a majority of the committee voted for the change. Eight Senate measures were amended on the floor of the House of Delegates, four of the amendments coming from committee members, three from other delegates, and one from an undiscovered source. There was, however, no committee opposition to any of them. Among the House bills in the same session, no amendments accepted by the House were offered by anyone save the author or a committee member. The Senate accepted three amendments offered from the floor by someone other than members of the committee. In two of these cases, the committee or a majority thereof, favored the amendment. In the third case the amendment was offered after the unfavorable report of the committee had been rejected. While no similar analysis was made of the amendments offered in the Pennsylvania legislature, general observation indicated that in large part, the amendments offered from the floor were there, likewise, either by the committee or with its approval or acceptance. The conclusion reached by the writer in this matter is that the action of the chambers in amending measures against the desires of the committee is practically negligible. Ultimately, the source of nearly all amendments will be found to be within the committee itself.

Sections V and VI on the tables are to show the further history of recommitted or re-referred bills. They make no appreciable change in the interpretations offered above but are included for sake of completing the bill histories. Group VII has no immediate relation to committee action and will be considered a few pages later. Section VIII, Table 16, discloses a rather curious practice. The bills, having received due consideration by committees of both houses and having passed the chambers themselves, might be thought to embody what the General Assembly wanted. Such a conclusion is too hasty. The records show that, of the 441 Senate bills sent to the governor, twenty-nine of them, or about one in fifteen, were recalled by the legislature. Twenty of these were amended and returned, six were returned without change, two were tabled and one was recommitted to perish. Of the 735 House bills submitted to the governor, thirty-seven, or about one in twenty, were recalled. Of these, twenty-seven were amended, one was returned without amendment and eight were tabled. In one case the governor refused to return the recalled bill. The extent of this recall practice indicates either a lack of careful consideration or a high degree of uncertainty on the part of the legislative bodies. To what amount the committees are responsible therefor is not known, but since, as has been shown, the houses accept almost without exception the committee proposals, here would seem to be a point of criticism upon committee action.

Mention was made in an earlier chapter [6] of a current practice in Maryland in the consideration of local measures. Since so many bills are referred to " select " committees as was there indicated,[7] attention should be given to their work. The accompanying table (No. 18) is based upon section III of Table 15. The columns headed " General " are the percentages given in Table 15 showing the nature of the committee reports on all bills referred. The columns headed " Local " show percentages of each kind of report based on all measures referred in Senate and House to the " select " committees. It is to be noted that in every case a higher percentage of " favorable " reports was returned than was true when all committee reports are considered. In fact, in all cases save that of House bills in the Senate, the percentage is markedly higher. In contrast the number of " no reports " is much smaller; that of " unfavorable " reports averages only

---

[6] See ch. ii.   [7] See p. 50.

TABLE 18. NATURE OF COMMITTEE REPORTS—LOCAL.

| | SENATE BILLS | | | | HOUSE BILLS | | | |
| | In Senate | | In House | | In House | | In Senate | |
	General[1]	Local	General[1]	Local	General[1]	Local	General[1]	Local
None	17.4	13.8	11.3	7.4	27.9	11.7	7.0	4.6
Favorable	55.5	69.7	76.2	83.7	51.3	75.1	73.8	76.1
Unfavorable	13.7	5.3	2.6	0.0	7.6	0.8	7.8	5.5
Fav. with amend.......	12.3	11.2	10.0	8.9	11.6	12.1	10.8	13.3
No. recommend.........	1.1	0.0	0.0	0.0	1.6	0.4	0.5	0.5

[1] Percentages in the columns headed "general" are based on all bills referred, including those to " select " committees.

slightly over one-third as much; while the percentage of amended reports is about the same.

One need not seek far for the explanation of these differences. In the first place the bills so considered are among their friends. The chairman of the Senate " select " committee is in most cases the author of the bill while the House delegation usually includes the author.[8] The county delegations with few exceptions are not politically divided. Such bills as are introduced " by request " may or may not receive much support in the committee. But, speaking generally, the individual senator and the local delegation in the House is left remarkably free to take care of local measures. The same statement holds true for the attitude of the houses toward such legislation. " If Alleghany County wants it, let her have it " is the prevalent feeling. About the only exceptions are found in bills having certain political angles and those dealing with prohibition matters. If the bill is actively opposed by a political faction in the county or Baltimore City, a division will appear in the legislature. Wet and dry measures may also bring a departure from the normal attitude. One can hardly expect one's belief in the political principle of county self-government to be superior to one's feeling on the wet and dry question. However, the same session that defeated a state-wide prohibition act by a vote of forty-five to sixty-four passed a dry measure applicable to

[8] This statement applies, of course, only while the bill is still in the house of origin.

Carroll County by a vote of sixty-five to forty-five and one for Frederick County by a similar majority. In explanation, some delegates declared they were voting " dry " not because they believed in prohibition but in line with the idea of home rule.

The net result of this practice would seem to be the placing of responsibility for local legislation almost wholly in the hands of the senator and the delegates—from two to six in number—from each county. Baltimore City, with its somewhat limited " Home Rule " charter, is not on a par with the counties in this matter. Is this procedure to be preferred to that of assigning local measures to standing committees according to subject matter? Should there be instead one or more general committees devoted to local measures? Or would log-rolling practices in either of these plans bring about the same final result without the responsibility which may be present in the Maryland scheme? The author suggests that county home-rule may be the advisable solution. The constitutional provisions to that end are not, however, very workable.[9] And, under the present system, the county often gets what it evidently does not want.[10] Whether that is more often true locally than generally is, however, unknown.

In an earlier connection,[11] the relation of administrative officers of the state to the committees was discussed. This subject merits further consideration. How do administrative measures fare in the committee room? An answer to that question may throw some light upon this relationship. In the 1929 sessions of both legislatures, the majority in both houses was in political agreement with the governor. On the other hand, in both cases, the 1929 session was the second in the governor's term when he is supposedly less powerful than in the preceding session. A former candidate for governor in Pennsylvania remarked that the legislature " eats out of the governor's hand " during his first session but becomes rather independent in the second. The success of administrative

---

[9] See H. W. Dodds, " A County Manager Charter in Maryland," National Municipal Review, IX, 505 ff.
[10] See ch. vi.   [11] See ch. iii.

measures, as shown in Table 19, indicates that in these two cases at any rate the administration exerted considerable influence even late in the gubernatorial term.

TABLE 19.   ADMINISTRATIVE MEASURES.[1]

| | PENNSYLVANIA | | | | MARYLAND | | | |
| | Adm. Bills | | All Bills | | | Adm. Bills | | All Bills | |
	No.	Per Cent.	Per Cent.	No.	No.	Per Cent.	Per Cent.	No.
Measures introduced...	162	100.0	100.0	2848	26	100.0	100.0	1059
House of origin								
Killed in committee..	19	11.7	50.3	1433	6	23.1	34.6	366
Amend. in committee.	33	20.4	15.9	452	9	31.2	12.3	130
Amend. by chamber..	42	25.9	7.5	214	1	3.8	2.9	31
Killed in chamber...	2	1.2	2.3	64	0	0.0	1.1	12
Passed by chamber..	141	87.0	47.4	1351	20	76.9	64.3	681
Second house [2]								
Killed in committee..	8	5.7	12.5	170	0	0.0	14.2	97
Amend. in committee.	25	17.7	13.4	183	2	10.0	11.2	76
Amend. by chamber..	33	23.4	7.9	107	1	5.0	2.9	20
Killed by chamber...	1	0.7	0.6	8	0	0.0	0.7	5
Passed by chamber..	132	93.6	86.9	1173	20	100.0	85.0	579
Sent to the Governor								
finally [3]............	132	81.5	41.2	1173	20	76.9	54.7	579

[1] For Pennsylvania, the bills here analyzed constitute most of the administrative proposals. A few more may have been introduced. For Maryland, measures sponsored by two departments only—Health and Conservation—are used, these being the only two in which it was possible to secure complete information.

[2] Percentages based on bills received by second House.

[3] Percentages based on measures introduced.

A glance at the columns of percentages shows some interesting contrasts between action taken upon administrative measures and all measures thrown together. In the first place, the committees kill less than one-fourth as many administrative measures as is true generally in the Pennsylvania houses of origin, and less than half as many in the second houses. A smaller contrast is seen in measures rejected by the chambers themselves. These are, however, rather insignificant in both cases. As to amendment, the administrative bills seem to be more often changed than is the case generally. This, however, can be explained in part. It being true that a much larger percentage of official bills is reported to the houses than of all bills, the chances for amendment both by the committees and by the chambers are increased. To illustrate the point, let us consider the third and fourth items. If the percentages there are computed upon the number of bills reported rather than upon those referred the following changes occur: 20.4 becomes 23.1; 15.9 becomes 31.9; 25.9 becomes 29.4; 7.5 becomes 15.1 In other words, committee amendment is actually less frequent on administrative bills although changes on them in the houses of origin remain more numerous. A similar situation exists in the second houses. The final comparison lies in the comparative number of bills finally sent to the governor. It is significant that the percentage of administrative measures finally submitted to the governor is nearly twice as large as is true of all measures considered indiscriminately.

The statistics included for Maryland are too incomplete to make the percentages at all accurate. But a similar tendency, although less pronounced, to favor bills sponsored by the administrative departments seems to exist. A much more thorough check of the Maryland situation would be necessary before making more definite conclusions. However, it takes no long acquaintance with Maryland legislation to appreciate the position of the governor. The individual departments may have some of their pet measures maltreated but it is generally recognized that the governor's legislative program receives generous approval. And, his relation to the legislature is quite as often marked by the killing of measures to which he is opposed as by the passage of those he wants.

This discussion of the history of bills sponsored by the administrative departments, combined with earlier observations [12] emphasizes the close relationship of what were intended, theoretically, to be independent departments. Part of the explanation is to be found doubtless in politics. The governor is in a position of political power with favors in his hands to bestow or withhold. The author's study, however, leads him to think that quite as much or more of it is a matter of leadership. The legislators follow the committees, particularly

---

[12] See ch. iii.

a few important ones. The committees in turn follow their chairmen, or their chairmen plus a few other members. The chairmen work in rather close co-operation with the administrative officers centering in the governor. Whether he gets his position as leader because his official position makes him more or less automatically so from a political angle or because of some other reason matters but little in this connection. The fact of administrative direction of legislation is evident.[13]

B. COMMITTEE ACTION AND BICAMERALISM

Some reference has been made in the preceding pages to comparative action on the part of the two houses, particularly with regard to committees. This is a convenient place to continue the discussion, noting the application of the bicameral principle and the governor's veto in comparison with the activity of the committees. The accompanying table (Number 20) attempts to present such comparisons for the 1929 session in Maryland and Pennsylvania in statistical form.

Thus tabulated, certain decided parallels and remarkable contrasts become at once evident. It is to be noted first that the action of the second house in killing bills is in both states strikingly similar. The Maryland Senate killed slightly more House bills than the House did those of the Senate— 15.4 per cent. to 14.5 per cent. In Pennsylvania, the percentages are reversed—12.6 per cent. for Senate action, 13.9 per cent. for the House. A similar situation is to be seen in the matter of amendment with a like reversal of percentages for the two states. Maryland's Senate amended 16.6 per cent. of all House bills passed by it; the House amended 15.0 per cent. of all the Senate bills it passed. The Pennsylvania percentages in the same order are 20.6 and 21.1. On the basis of these figures neither house in either state can claim a superior position as the people's watch-dog.

---

[13] Cf. Legislative Voters' League, Assembly Bulletin, August 21, 1925, regarding wholesale passage of administrative measures in Illinois.

The number of bills killed in the house of origin varies more than the above as between House and Senate, although not strikingly dissimilar. In Maryland the Senate killed 31.5 per cent. of its own bills, the House 38.9 per cent. of its own. The Pennsylvania percentages in the same order are 45.6 and 56.0. In both states the House is more deadly as to its own offspring than as to its nieces. As to amendment, the

TABLE 20. COMMITTEE ACTION, BICAMERALISM, AND VETO.[1]

| | SENATE | | | | HOUSE | | | |
	Senate Bills No.	Per Cent.	House Bills No.	Per Cent.	House Bills No.	Per Cent.	Senate Bills No.	Per Cent.
I. Maryland, 1929								
Bills referred	453		370		606		311	
Bills killed by committee [2]..	137	30.2	53	14.3	229	37.8	44	14.1
Bills killed by chamber [3]...	5	1.1	4	1.1	7	1.2	1	0.3
Bills killed, total..........	142	31.3	57	15.4	236	38.9	45	14.5
Bills passed, total.........	311	68.7	313	84.6	370	61.1	266	85.5
Passed bills amended by com.	61	19.6	41	13.1	69	18.6	35	13.2
Passed bills amended by chamber [4]..............	22	7.1	12	3.8	9	2.4	8	3.0
Passed bills amended, total.	79	25.4	52	16.6	76	20.5	40	15.0
Bills sent to governor.....	266	58.6			313	51.7		
Bills vetoed by governor...	14	5.3			44	14.1		
II. Pennsylvania, 1929								
Bills referred	935		850		1913		512	
Bills killed by committee..	420 [5]	44.9	104	12.2	1013	53.0	66	12.9
Bills killed by chamber [6]...	6 [7]	0.6	3	0.4	58 [8]	3.0	5	1.0
Bills killed, total..........	426	45.6	107	12.6	1071	56.0	71	13.9
Bills passed, total	509	54.4	743	87.4	842	44.0	441	86.1
Passed bills amended by com.	181	35.6	116	15.6	271	32.2	67	15.2
Passed bills amended by chamber [4]..............	76	14.9	59	7.9	138	16.4	48	10.9
Passed bills amended, total.	231	45.4	153	20.6	377	44.8	93	21.1
Bills sent to governor [9]....	438	46.8			735	38.4		
Bills vetoed by governor...	80	18.3			131	17.8		

[1] Compiled from same data as Tables 14, 15, and 16, and from veto messages of two governors.
[2] Includes " unfavorable " reports accepted by the chambers. Recommitted bills are also included if killed by committee.
[3] " No action " bills which had been reported unfavorably, not included.
[4] See explanation on page 114, above, indicating that these percentages are really too high.
[5] Includes one measure recalled from the governor.
[6] Includes " dropped " bills.
[7] Includes two measures recalled from governor.
[8] Includes eight measures recalled from governor.
[9] Does not include those recalled.

Maryland Senate acted upon 25.4 per cent. of its own passed measures, the House upon 20.5 per cent. of passed bills originating there. The similar Pennsylvania percentages are 45.4 and 44.8. A certain amount of this higher rate in the latter state is to be accounted for by amendments to appropriation bills, apparently more often amended than other measures. The absence of a large number of such bills in Maryland under the budget system pares down the percentages somewhat.

The contrasts spoken of are to be seen first in the relative casualty rate as between committee and chamber. Comparatively speaking, the chambers themselves kill an insignificant number of bills, the only item of considerable size being noted in the case of the fifty-eight House bills killed by the Pennsylvania House. This included, however, as indicated in Table 16, at least thirty-four measures " dropped " without any apparent committee opposition. Recalling the discussion above,[14] we note that the contrast is even greater than the table percentages show. The earlier discussion of the source of amendments [15] indicates that the percentages given in the later table show considerably less contrast than is actually the case.

One further comparison remains. This involves the matter of the governor's veto. A legitimate comparison would seem to be one between the rate of negative action by the second house and of veto, based in each case upon the number of bills presented. Maryland's governor vetoed 5.3 per cent. of all Senate bills presented to him as compared to the House negative action of 13.2 per cent. Of House bills, the governor vetoed 14.1 per cent. as compared to 15.4 per cent. killed by the Senate. Putting these together, it is seen that the second house killed approximately 15.0 per cent.[16] of all bills received from the houses of origin, while the governor vetoed 10.0 per cent. of all bills sent to him. Examination of the

---

[14] See pp. 112 ff.
[15] See pp. 114 ff.
[16] This figure would be slightly decreased by the elimination of duplicate bills, the killing of which constitutes no real check.

1927 records, however, disclose a somewhat higher veto rate. The House of Delegates killed that year 16.2 per cent. of all Senate bills reaching it, while the governor vetoed 8.9 per cent. Of the House bills, the Senate killed 18.7 per cent. of all sent to it and the governor vetoed 15.8 per cent. of all reaching him. The second houses therefore took negative action on approximately 16.4 per cent. of all bills sent to them as compared to vetoes of the governor amounting to 12.6 per cent.

Comparative statistics for Pennsylvania reveal a much higher veto rate. Whereas the second houses in the two states killed approximately the same share of bills coming from the houses of origin, the veto rate for Pennsylvania is markedly higher than for Maryland. The Pennsylvania Senate refused passage for 12.6 per cent. of House bills reaching it, the governor vetoed 17.8 per cent. Among Senate bills, the House negatived 13.9 per cent.; the vetoes of the governor amounted to 18.3 per cent. Using the second houses together, they negatived 13.1 per cent. of all bills coming from the houses of origin; the governor vetoed 18.0 per cent. of all bills coming to him from the legislature.

What conclusions may be drawn from the above? Certainly, with information over such a temporary period, any general conclusions as to either the efficiency of committee systems or the effects of bicameralism would be wholly unjustified. However, certain observations may be permitted. One tendency stands out preeminently: the sifting and revisory processes belong to the committees, only in a minor degree to the chambers themselves. That the committees in the houses of origin perform the major part of this work is evident. However, a great deal of it is done in the second house committees and raises the question of the advisability of abolishing bicameralism. The lower rate in the second house is, of course, partly due to the fact that the worst bills have already been eliminated. On the other hand, the necessity for second house action seems often to be based upon the good American policy of " passing the buck " or upon the idea that the second house will take care of the minor errors. As an illustration of the shifting of responsibility, a case in the Maryland House of Delegates is recalled. A bill had been reported unfavorably from committee. The majority and minority floor leaders united in opposition to its passage by the House. They even went to the extreme of suggesting that here was merely a case of " passing the buck " to the Senate. But, due partly to the Speaker's support (dictated, it was said, by personal attitude toward the author), partly out of regard for the author by the delegates, and partly, without doubt, because of endorsement of the idea of the bill, it passed. It then became necessary for the Senate to destroy it or, in turn, to " pass the buck " to the governor. The committee brought in an unfavorable report. The Senate substituted the bill for the report and passed the measure, but with an amendment which seemed to make it harmless. In that form it became law. Had no second house existed, the writer is convinced that the House of Delegates would not have acted as it did, at least not without greater deliberation. Observation indicated, too, that the second house often gives but casual consideration to measures. As has been indicated above,[17] the amount of time allowed is often slight because of the lateness of receipt. Sometimes it is caused by mere postponement. The clerk of one of the two major Maryland House committees reported on March 21, 1929—nine days before the end of the session—that no action had yet been taken by the committee on any Senate bill. But not infrequently in committee meetings such comment as the following is heard:

. . . This bill was thoroughly considered in the other house. There seems to be nothing wrong with it. Let's report it favorably.

Many times, doubtless, the " thorough consideration " in the other house was of the variety of " There doesn't seem to be anything wrong with this. Let's report it out." With such procedure, the check of the second house ceases to be a check and the whole legislative process becomes merely a matter of unanimous consent. Strikingly " vicious " bills may be stopped.

---

[17] See p. 105.

At the same time much more or less useless legislation is enacted.

The governor's veto emerges, so far as the above evidence extends, as an important check upon legislation. That the veto rate upon bills which have undergone two siftings should be comparable with the negative action of the second house seems remarkable. May not a more careful, responsible consideration by one house plus gubernatorial action constitute about as guarded a process of legislation as the bicameral system [18] now in vogue?

---

[18] More complete studies of the bicameral system in operation are to be seen in David Leigh Colvin, The Bicameral Principle in the New York Legislature (New York, 1913); Dorothy Schaffter, The Bicameral System in Practice (Iowa City, Iowa, 1929); James Allan Clifford Grant, The Bicameral Principle in the California Legislature (unpublished Leland Stanford Jr. University thesis); May Wood-Simons, "The Operation of the Bicameral System in Illinois and Wisconsin," in the Illinois Law Review, XX, 674; and John E. Hall, "The Bicameral Principle in the New Mexico Legislature," in the National Municipal Review, XVI, 185, 255.

CHAPTER VI

EVALUATION OF COMMITTEE SYSTEMS

The foregoing chapters have been concerned with a description of the committee systems in Maryland and Pennsylvania, together with an analysis of their organization, procedure and product. Can committee efficiency in these legislatures be evaluated? If one could set up a standard measuring-stick alongside each system and take its measure in understandable units, the task would be comparatively easy. Lacking such, however, some tests may still be applied. The present chapter is in part an attempt to apply certain tests, objective and otherwise, which indicate somewhat of the effectiveness of the committee systems.

A. OBJECTIVE TESTS

1. Repeals and Amendments of Recent Legislation.

Since the committees are so largely responsible for what appears on the statute books,[1] it would seem that the subsequent changes of legislative enactments bear some relation to the committee system. Why are such changes made? In part, they are to correct technical errors in the laws: faulty construction, incorrect references or names, ambiguities, etc. Partially they represent the effect of more or less experimental legislation. In certain cases a change of conditions may make amendment or repeal advisable. Occasionally an interpretation of the court makes new legislation necessary to accomplish the desired result. And it may well be that public opinion sometimes shifts from one position to another, demanding change. An important cause in recent sessions in both Maryland and Pennsylvania lies in the codification or re-codification of laws in many fields.[2]

To what extent may the causes of change be connected with committee action? Certainly an altered public opinion is quite beyond committee control. But comparatively few laws

---

[1] See ch. v.
[2] In Ohio the blame for a similar situation is placed upon inexperienced legislators acting "without adequate study or technical advice." Civic League of Cleveland, Civic Affairs, No. 21 (1919).

are so affected and such effects as may be found are usually
the result of many years rather than few. If the legislation
is of an experimental nature, the testing period should be
over several years' time and immediate change would seem
inadvisable. Conditions necessitating changes of laws are
likewise apt to be slow of alteration so that amendments and
repeals from this cause should not be at all immediate in
most cases. Court interpretations, too, are responsible for
only occasional changes. These interpretations themselves,
moreover, constitute a certain criticism of the legislative act.
There remains undoubtedly a considerable field of legislative
alteration not caused by any of the factors just mentioned. It
would be impossible to measure quantitatively the exact
relation between the quality of committee product and the
changes thereof in immediately subsequent sessions. There
would seem to be, however, some significance in the information contained in Table 21. This indicates the changes,
made in the three most recent sessions of the Pennsylvania
and Maryland legislatures, of acts passed by the three immediately preceding sessions. In other words the one hundred and fifty-five acts repealed in Pennsylvania are made up
of 1929 acts repealing laws of 1927, 1925 and 1923, of 1927
acts repealing laws of 1925, 1923 and 1921, and of 1925 acts
repealing laws of 1923, 1921 and 1919. The remainder of
the table is constructed similarly.

TABLE 21. REPEALS AND AMENDMENTS OF RECENT LEGISLATION.[1]
(*Affecting Acts of Three Preceding Sessions.*)

	PENNSYLVANIA		MARYLAND	
	Total	Average	Total	Average
Repeals of acts....................	155	51.7	17	5.7
Amendments to acts...............	565[2]	188.3	217	72.3
Number of acts passed (five sessions affected)	2266[3]	453.2	3127	625.4
Percentage of acts repealed within three sessions		11.4		0.9
Percentage of acts amended within three sessions		41.5		11.6
Percentage of acts amended or re-pealed within three sessions......		52.9		12.5

[1] Compiled from Maryland and Pennsylvania Session Laws.
[2] Includes 59 partial repeals. The 1929 session also amended 24
of its own measures.   [3] Disregarding appropriation acts.

The legislature of Pennsylvania, according to this table, repeals within three sessions 11.4 per cent. of its enactments. At that rate it would in a little over fifty years repeal all its statute law. It amends or partially repeals, moreover, 41.5 per cent. of its laws within three subsequent sessions. Six sessions would suffice, if the rate be maintained, to alter (amend or repeal) the entire statutory law, providing, of course, that the alterations be scattered over the entire body of the laws. A study in Massachusetts in 1915 [3] revealed that 30 per cent. of all laws passed by the General Court are affected by legislation within the next three sessions. This was considered to be a condition demanding attention, the report stating:

. . . While it is not likely that any method can be found which will entirely eliminate such evils, still, anything which will tend to decrease the number of so-called ' perfecting-amendment ' bills . . . will be welcomed.[4]

In Massachusetts there were, of course, annual sessions, so the 30 per cent. alteration may be somewhat commensurate with the 52.9 per cent. noted above in Pennsylvania.

It might be suggested that a change in legislative personnel may be responsible for much of the alteration. Statistics do not so indicate. The 1929 session contained only sixty-four new representatives in a total of two hundred eight and six new senators in a total of fifty. The same political party retained control. But this session repealed nineteen acts passed in 1927 and amended or partly repealed ninety-five. In addition it repealed two and amended twenty-four of its own acts to say nothing of recalling sixty-six measures from the governor for purposes of amending or defeating. It must be said in partial explanation of the rapid rate of repeal that the codification mentioned above has had considerable effect. The 1929 session passed eight laws which may be classified as codes. A check upon the effects of these acts reveals that they

---

[3] Report of the Joint Special Committee on Legislative Procedure, January, 1915. The percentage is computed on the basis of a table on page 46, so as to be comparable to the statistics in Table 21.
[4] Ibid., p. 47.

9

repealed forty-six laws passed by the three preceding sessions. Table 21 shows that there were sixty-six repeals over the same period. There remain repeals by this session of twenty recent laws unexplained by the codifying process. This number is practically the same as that disclosed in the Massachusetts study. A legislative system which requires, or at least results in, so much change would seem to need careful examination. Wholly aside from personnel, a revamping of the committee system so as to secure or make possible more careful consideration of proposed legislation might diminish the rather unstable condition of the laws indicated above.

How may one account for the lower rate of change in Maryland? The higher number of acts passed in each session —625.4 as compared to 453.2—is largely explained by the very large amount of local legislation in Maryland. That in turn means that the base, on which the percentages are calculated, is larger. But the local legislation would seem to need change quite as often as the general. In fact, out of forty-three 1927 measures amended in the 1929 session, twenty-eight were local measures. The greater tendency in Pennsylvania to continue the same legislators in office ought seemingly to result in greater stability of legislation, rather than in the more rapid change noted. Conceivably, there is in Maryland a greater conservatism, a desire to allow laws to remain as they are. Possibly there is in Pennsylvania more careful inspection of the laws so as to determine the need for amendment or repeal while in Maryland the errors of legislation remain. But the marked tendency in the former state to amend acts of the current session (twenty-four cases in 1929 as well as two repeals) and the frequent requests to the governor to return bills once passed (sixty-six instances in 1929) indicates sufficient laxity in legislation to explain somewhat the high amending rate shown in the table.

Whatever the explanation of rapid alteration or the variation between the two states may be, the tendency toward frequent change of recent legislation constitutes undoubtedly a criticism of legislative procedure. If any reorganization of committees or use of expert assistance can contribute to the laws a character making for greater stability, such reform deserves adoption.

2. Governor's Vetoes.

The veto messages of the governor constitute another possible test of the efficiency of the legislative process. Fortunately, in both Maryland and Pennsylvania, the governor's reasons for disapproval of legislative enactments are available. The Constitution of the latter state provides that bills sent to the governor during the last ten days of the session shall become laws unless filed, along with the objections thereto, in the office of the Secretary of the Commonwealth within thirty days of adjournment.[5] These objections, together with veto messages sent during the session, are published by the Commonwealth. Maryland has no similar provision, but the present governor has followed the practice of writing his objections to all bills disapproved. These are published with the session laws.

An examination of these veto messages in the two states for the regular sessions of 1927 and 1929 reveals the information tabulated in Table 22. So far as possible all vetoes based upon a difference of policy between the governor and the legislature have been eliminated. What remains constitutes seemingly a criticism of the legislative process. Included among others under the heading " Unnecessary " are enactments repeating laws already on the statute books or granting powers where they already exist. The " Duplication " item includes identical or nearly identical measures and special or local acts covered by more general ones. These are confined to duplicate provisions within the output of the same session. The " Vague, Careless, Ambiguous, etc." heading covers a multitude of legislative sins. Bad wording, internal inconsistency, insufficient or incorrect titles, failure of the legislation to accomplish what was apparently intended—these are some of the reasons for veto included here.

----

[5] Art. IV, Sec. 15.

TABLE 22. GOVERNORS' VETOES.

	MARYLAND		PENNSYLVANIA	
	1927	1929	1927	1929
Reasons for Veto				
Unnecessary	12	6	8	8
Duplication	16	17	20	40
Unconstitutional	6	6	13	21
Inconsistent with another act of same session	1	1	6	13
Formerly repealed or antedated......	0	0	1	15
Affecting a repealed or non-existent act.	2	0	0	1
Vague, careless, ambiguous, etc.......	6	5	5	6
Total	43	35	53	104
Total of all vetoes...............	92	58	177	211
Percentage of vetoes on grounds other than policy......................	46.7	60.3	29.9	49.3
Average for the two sessions..........	58.5		39.6	

A committee system which permits the enactment of from thirty-five to forty-three, or from fifty-three to one hundred four defective laws needs attention. It is hardly possible that so many vetoes would be necessary if really " careful consideration " were given to the bills by the committees receiving them. Some quotations from the veto messages indicate how careless the legislative process often is.

. . . It is apparent that the bill was hastily drawn . . . Some of the provisions are more or less vague and uncertain.

. . . If this bill were approved, it would not be possible to hold any future elections for city councilmen in Hagerstown, because the years therefor are left blank and unspecified.

. . . The bill was defectively drawn, and those interested requested its veto.

. . . This bill has no enacting clause.

. . . This bill . . . was only introduced about two weeks before the close of the session, and I have been advised of a number of ambiguities and conflicts with the provisions of the charter of Cumberland which are contained in the bill.

. . . Section 2 of the act, which provides for penalties, is unconstitutional, as the title of the act does not give notice that penalties are provided for therein. While in all probability Section 2 is the only section of the act which would be declared unconstitutional because of the defect in the title, it would be useless to approve the act as it would be incapable of enforcement.

. . . This bill does not designate the persons or officials of the counties who may incur the expenses, the nature of the expenditures, or the persons by whom or to whom verified accounts of such expenditures are to be submitted.

. . . The title of this bill recites that it is an amendment to Section 20 of the act of June 2, 1891, P. L. 176. As a matter of fact, the bill is intended to amend Section 14 of Article II of such act, which latter section was amended by Section 20 of the act of June 8, 1901, P. L. 535.

. . . This bill is loosely drawn and would render it a criminal offense for any person to give away without any false pretense of any character, artificial flowers.

. . . The present bill would add certain words to the Act of 1927 which would make it impossible for anyone by any process of interpretation to determine what this language means.[6]

With the legislative assistance offered in each state by the Legislative Reference Bureau, careful committee work should avoid a major part of such errors. It is hardly fair to the governor to place upon him the responsibility of vetoing, for the reasons here indicated, what may otherwise be meritorious legislation.

3. Duplicate Bills.

The practice of introducing duplicate bills affords another means of testing the committee systems objectively. In both Maryland and Pennsylvania a considerable number of identical Senate and House bills are introduced at each session. An examination of their history illustrates something of the functioning of the committee system. This is particularly true of the reference of bills as summarized in Table 23. This shows for Maryland information on all the duplicate bills introduced in the last two sessions. No ready means was found for discovering similar data in Pennsylvania, but, on the fifteen pairs which reached the governor as identical enactments, some facts of their legislative history are recorded.

The fact that the two legislatures have, in large part, similar committees in the two houses makes possible a more detailed comparison of the reference of bills, than would be true otherwise. It is to be noted in item (a) that approximately one-fourth of the Maryland pairs of bills and nearly one-half of

---

[6] These quotations are from messages of Maryland's governor in 1924, 1927, and 1929, and from those of Pennsylvania's governor in 1927 and 1929.

those in Pennsylvania received a dissimilar reference in their houses of origin. For instance, Senate Bill 45 was referred to the Senate committee on Judicial Proceedings while its companion, House Bill 36, went to the House committee on Hygiene. A second comparison, and more valuable as a test, is to be seen in items (b) and (c). In the reference of the House bills to Senate committees and of Senate bills to House committees a rather marked diversity is noted. In Maryland approximately one-fifth of such references were to committees other than those receiving the companion measure. The Pennsylvania variation, in the limited scope of the data, is considerably greater, forty per cent. of the bills having been referred to different committees. Items (d) and (e) reveal another and very interesting comparison. There seems to be a tendency to refer a measure in the second house to the same committee which received it in the house of origin whether or not that agrees with the earlier reference of the duplicate bill. Thus in Maryland, combining the numbers

TABLE 23. DUPLICATE BILLS.[1]

		MARYLAND		PENNSYLVANI
		1927	1929	1929
	No. of pairs of duplicate bills introduced..........	51	59	15
a	No. of pairs referred to similar committees in houses of origin [2]	38	46	8
	No. of pairs referred to dissimilar committees....	13	13	7
b	No. of pairs referred to same Senate committees....	14	18	9
	No. of pairs referred to different Senate committees.	5	4	6
c	No. of pairs referred to same House committees....	30	19	9
	No. of pairs referred to different House committees..	6	5	6
d	No. of Senate bills referred to similar committees in House as in Senate.........................	33	20	11
	No. of Senate bills referred to dissimilar committees in House as in Senate.........................	3	4	4
e	No. of House bills referred to similar committees in Senate as in House...........................	12	20	9
	No. of House bills referred to dissimilar committees in Senate as in House.........................	7	2	6
	No. of duplicate bills passed by both Senate and House	50	35	
	No. of pairs passed by both Senate and House.....	8	6	15
	Resulting number of laws.......................	43 [3]	29	

[1] Based on same sources as Tables 14, 15 and 16, above.
[2] Wherever bills received double reference, both committees were considered in making comparisons.
[3] Includes two identical laws.

in the two items, eighty-five measures out of one hundred one, or more than five-sixths, were so referred. In Pennsylvania, two-thirds of the references followed the example of the other house.

In addition to the identical measures in Pennsylvania cited above, other duplications are disclosed in the governor's veto messages. In eight instances, Senate and House bills sent to the governor covered the same subject matter. The reference of these measures follows very closely what was disclosed in items (b) and (c) above but with a greater tendency toward similarity of reference in the houses of origin. There were also eight appropriation bills, four from each house, covered as to subject matter by general appropriation acts. These had similar references throughout, all being assigned to Appropriations committees in both houses. They represent, therefore, a complete duplication of effort although consistent in reference. The governor's veto messages further reveal certain duplication in bills originating in the same house. For this cause, he vetoed three Senate bills as covered by three other Senate measures and eight House bills whose provisions were found in eight others. In the houses of origin one Senate pair out of three and two House pairs out of eight showed dissimilar reference. Two Senate pairs out of three and six House pairs out of eight received the same commitment in the second house. Out of twenty-two chances, bills were sent to the same committee in both houses in twelve instances, to different ones in ten. So far, therefore, as reference of measures is concerned, no marked change in the situation described above is brought about by these special groups of duplicates.

What conclusions may be drawn from the data given above? In addition to the more general criticism of bill references in a former chapter,[7] the present information discloses a remarkable inconsistency. That the same presiding officers should send identical measures to different committees in one case in five in Maryland and more than twice as often

---

[7] See ch. iii.

in Pennsylvania is indicative at least of considerable uncertainty. Such a practice necessitates, in the case of companion bills, a duplication of effort on the part of committees and, to the extent that careful consideration prevails, a waste of time. If the same uncertain reference occurs in other measures, duplication of effort will also occur because Senate and House bills, similar but not identical, are bound to be introduced. The scope of each committee's activities should be so defined as to eliminate so great an amount of inconsistent reference. Possibly a committee on reference, as found in some legislatures, could handle the matter more efficiently. A reorganization of committee alignment so as to avoid overlapping wherever possible is also recommended.

A more careful examination of the history of these duplicate measures might reveal other interesting data on committee action. For instance, it is sometimes found that one member of the pair has been amended and the other one not or that a committee or different committees of the same house have taken different action on the two bills. The materials for such a study, however, are not readily available. But the mere fact of the passage of identical measures as indicated in the tables is in itself somewhat of a criticism of committees. The California rules provide that either house may substitute one companion measure for the other, thus eliminating duplication of effort.[8] It seems probable, however, that the effectiveness of such a rule would depend in part upon consistent reference. Perhaps the use of joint committees would avoid unnecessary duplication here as it pretends to do generally.

It must be said, however, that duplication and even uncertainty are not wholly due to careless, improper, or inconsistent reference. Pennsylvania's governor vetoed thirteen measures in 1929 as being inconsistent with other measures passed by the same session. Examination of the reference of these bills reveals that more than a third of these inconsis-

---

[8] " But few companion bills are ever substituted in file, as provided in the rules." James A. C. Grant, The Bicameral Principle in California (unpublished), p. 127.

tencies came from the same committee in House or Senate.
It is quite impossible to determine the cause of such action.
In some cases, however, the inconsistency was conscious. For
instance, the Senate Committee on Repeal Bills reported
favorably on Senate Bill No. 9 and House Bill No. 131 on
the same day. One of these provided for immediate and the
other for graduated repeal of the tax on anthracite coal. The
committee's purpose was undoubtedly to permit, or compel
the governor to select one or the other of the proposals. This
could be either a shifting of responsibility, or a grant of
power to the governor to adjust revenues to expenditures. In
several instances a like spirit was witnessed in committee
meetings—let the governor select whichever one he wants.
Where such committee actions are conscious, there may be
certain arguments favorable to them. But the unconscious
inconsistencies, whether due to the fact that different committees have acted upon the bills or to lack of careful consideration by the committee receiving both bills, constitute a
valid criticism of the committee system as applied. And the
governor's veto is no answer. He is unable to veto the inconsistent portions and approve the remainder. His power is
not one of amendment, but of negation. And the meritorious
provisions of a bill suffer the same fate as those which necessitate the veto.

The Massachusetts committee referred to above suggested
a special official to see to these very aspects of legislation.
The report reads:

. . . Each act should be carefully tested as to its harmony and co-
ordination with existing law, to see whether it is a duplicate of any
other law or is inconsistent with any, or does in another way what
is already done in one way. The provision of the act should be
clearly adequate to its purpose without accomplishing something
never intended.[9]

With the mass of proposed legislation confronting present-
day legislative committees, the avoidance of duplication and
inconsistency is a matter for the expert. The committee
itself cannot be held entirely responsible. One feels, however, that even with the present machinery, some improve-

---

[9] Op. cit., p. 51.

ments might be had through more careful committee
consideration.

4. The Referendum.

The Constitution of Maryland provides for a referendum
of legislative acts upon petition of the voters. This is made
applicable to measures affecting individual counties as well as
to state-wide laws. To date it has been used only on local
measures. Recalling the Maryland procedure in legislating
for local units,[10] the results of the application of the referendum may have certain significance in testing its efficiency.

Presumably Anne Arundel County gets by way of local
legislation what Anne Arundel County wants. But the
statistical information contained in Table 24 throws doubt
upon the accuracy of that presumption. Out of twenty
county measures referred by petition in four elections,
eighteen were rejected, usually by overwhelming votes. The
two accepted were by narrow margins,—of 176 in one case

TABLE 24. REFERENDUM IN MARYLAND.[1]

Year	Chap. No.	For	Against	Year	Chap. No.	For	Against
1920....	291	1122	2425	1927....	48	1167	7245
	320	806	2374		231	1287	7509
	386	2782	2606		241	1183	7426
1922....	199	1729	3278		264	292	2084
	340	1657	2633		271	1253	7821
	498	2348	2313		275	1214	7401
	524	1937	2967		388	1189	7386
1924....	74	5041	7275		392	1266	7419
	75	4199	7816		422	1229	7530
					523	1260	7526
					579	1500	3020

Total number of acts referred.............................. 20
Number of acts rejected................................... 18

Total vote: For—34,461; Against—106,054.
Negative vote, percentage of total—75 plus.

[1] Information tabulated from reports of the Secretary of State,
included in Maryland Session Laws, 1922, 1924, 1927, 1929.

and of 35 in the other. As is indicated in the table, the
negative vote on all measures referred amounted to more than

[10] See chs. ii and v.

three-fourths of the total vote cast. While the number of
measures referred is of course small, there seems to be some
significance in these rejections. A committee system, intended
to represent the local communities, should reflect local desires
more accurately than is indicated in many cases. An extreme
opposition of seven to one in one instance and an average of
three to one in all measures referred suggests the need of some
more accurate method of giving expression to local public
opinion.

B. Theoretical Evaluation

What are the functions of legislative committees? Quite
obviously, the rating to be given to a system depends on how
well it fulfills its function. If the Maryland and Pennsylvania committee systems are to be evaluated, their raison d'etre
must be first determined. Neither legislature has avowedly
made any attempt to define the functions of the committees.
A careful reading of their rules, however, combined with
observation as to their practice may be enlightening, particularly as they modify theoretical discussions of committee
functions.

Committees in legislative bodies vary widely as to their
purposes. The committees of the House of Commons,[11] for
instance, have no counterpart in American state legislatures.
Neither do the states agree as to the proper role of committees.[12] In some cases they are looked upon more or less as
advisory groups wherein specialized knowledge may be applied
to technical questions. Elsewhere they have been granted or
have assumed a position of " little legislatures " using their
privileged positions to control law-making. These variations
make difficult a precise and universal definition of committee
functions and help to explain, doubtless, the differences of
opinion expressed by writers on the subject.

In his study of the committee system in Iowa, Horack says:

. . . The chief function of a legislative committee is to investigate,
consider or deliberate upon and then make recommendations to the
house concerning the subjects referred to it.[13]

---

[11] See Robert Luce, Legislative Procedure (N. Y., 1922), pp. 183 ff.
[12] See Arthur N. Holcombe, State Government in the United States
(New York, 1926), pp. 261 ff.   [13] Op. cit., p. 561

Referring to the committee system as organized in America, Luce [14] writes: " The other idea was that a few members should advise the whole as to purpose or policy and as to how it would best be accomplished." Later he refers to the work of a committee as being " merely advisory and not binding." Despite these expressions, however, the general tenor of his discussion would give the committees much wider power than " merely advisory." He would permit committees to pigeon-hole bills to which the committee was unanimously opposed.[15] Perhaps as satisfactory a definition as any is the one given by Dodd:

. . . The true function of a legislative committee is to prepare business for and to recommend action by the larger body of which the committee is theoretically an agent.[16]

It is to be noticed that in none of these, save in an extremely mild form in Luce, is there any suggestion of the existence of committees as " sifting " agencies. In all three cases, reports to the parent body seem to be taken for granted.

An analysis of these definitions indicates that the committee should be an agent of the legislative body for the following purposes:

1.   To serve as a means of investigating special fields of proposed legislation and collecting information thereon;

2.   To deliberate upon (more time being available than in the chamber itself) and give careful consideration to matters referred to it;

3.   To permit the application of specialized knowledge so that proposed legislation may be in such a form as to accomplish the desired end and that the chamber may benefit by more or less expert advise;

4.   Finally, to recommend action.

The function of sifting the measures referred, reporting only on those favored by the committee or certain members thereof, in order to expedite the business of the legislative body, may

---

[14] Op. cit., pp. 102, 108.
[15] Ibid., p. 166.
[16] Walter F. Dodd, State Government (New York, 1928), p. 184.

be added. The procedural and administrative funtions of some standing committees are omitted since they have formed no part of the present study.

To what extent do the legislatures of Maryland and Pennsylvania, at least in theory, accept the above statement of committee functions? First of all, the fact that committees are recognized as agents is attested by rules governing their appointment, their reports, their method of discharge from further consideration of a bill, and in Pennsylvania, their records; all of these have received attention in the earlier chapters. An attempted specialization of fields is indicated by the very names of the committees in both states and by provisions to refer measures to " appropriate " committees. Greater deliberation than the chamber could give is implied in the constitutional provision in Pennsylvania that " No bill shall be considered unless referred to a committee . . . . " [17] Maryland House Rule 55 provides that " All resolutions and orders . . . [with certain exceptions] . . . shall be referred to their appropriate committees." The Senate rule [18] reads:

. . . Upon the introduction of each Bill or Joint Resolution it shall be read the first time and then referred by the President to its appropriate committee, unless otherwise ordered.

A later rule makes similar provisions for House Bills reaching the Senate. It may be noted that these Maryland rules imply also committee specialization as do similar rules in Pennsylvania regarding reference to " appropriate committees." Specialization, permitting expert advice, is further indicated by the tendency, more pronounced in Pennsylvania than in Maryland, to continue the same members on the same committees over a number of sessions. The rules of both Maryland houses make it the duty of committees to report all measures referred, providing an easy means of discharge if no report appears within a limited time. In Pennsylvania, on the other hand, the sifting function of committees is clearly recognized, the discharge rule particularly in the House being intended apparently to permit pigeon-holing rather than to prevent

---

[17] Art. III, Sec. 2.   [18] Rule 21, Sec. 5.

it. Whether this is a legitimate committee function in its present form is a debatable matter.

If the functions of committees outlined above be accepted, what are the desiderata in a committee system to perform them? And how do the two systems considered in this study measure up to them? The two questions can be more conveniently answered jointly. And, since the desirable features to be discussed are often related to more than one of the functions and *vice versa,* they will be here considered after the order of earlier chapters of this study.

In the first place, how can committee composition be made to serve the functions outlined? If special fields of legislation are to be investigated, the range of committees should reflect the existence of those special fields. That such is not entirely the case in either state is shown partially at least by the existence of many useless or nearly useless committees. To be sure, the rating of a committee by the number of bills referred to it may be a doubtful method, since the criticism may be of the reference of bills rather than of the range of committees. However, no reason is apparent for the continuance of such committees as those on Insolvency, Internal Improvements, and Currency in the Maryland House; or of those on Canals and Inland Navigation in the Pennsylvania Senate, and on Geological Survey and Bureau of Statistics in the House. A revamping of the committee system so as to more nearly agree with the legislative fields existent in the two states is in order. This should be based upon a careful study over a number of sessions of the nature of proposed legislation. Whether the reorganized administrative departments may serve as a guide in determining the committees necessary, as has been suggested in some states,[19] is problematical. The fact that Maryland's reorganization leaves much to be desired in the way of departmentalization of related administrative agencies sheds doubt upon the value of such a suggestion in that state. That a realignment, combining present committees in related fields, is not only possible but advisable in both

---

[19] See, for instance, "The Legislative Department," Illinois Constitutional Convention Bulletins, No. 8.

states, however, is quite apparent. Such changes as are made should, moreover, aim to decrease materially the number of committees in all four of the chambers.

In line with such reorganization, the selection of committee members should serve the purposes of specialization. In so far as continuity of committee service indicates an attempt to benefit from the specialized knowledge of committee members, the Pennsylvania practice must be commended. On the other hand, the shifting of committee positions in the Maryland House of Delegates, combined with the total disuse of the abilities of certain delegates, disregards the benefits to be derived from specialization. The existence of a large number of committees with the necessary accompaniment of multiple committee assignments, a situation aggravated by large committee size in Pennsylvania, means less possibility of specialized knowledge and expert advice. A selection of committee members on the basis of special abilities and a severe cutting down of the number of committee assignments for each member should go along with the revamping of committee fields discussed above.

Still a third feature of committee composition seems highly desirable if specialization and careful consideration are to result. Committee sizes should be strictly limited. This is necessary in order to permit attendance upon committee meetings and hearings, an impossibility under a system of multiple assignments. It would seem also to be desirable in order to serve the function of deliberation. Committees of nine members deliberate more efficiently than those of thirty. If committees are to recommend action and their advice is to be as often accepted as appears evident, careful consideration of measures is necessary. Since comparatively small committees then seem advisable, what may be said of the systems under consideration? The Pennsylvania committees are too large. An average size of nearly nineteen in the Senate and more than thirty in the House, with resulting average assignments of thirteen and six and-a-half respectively, means, necessarily, conflicting committee meetings, a disintegration of whatever specialized knowledge exists, and less careful consideration of measures than would be possible under a reorganized system. In Maryland, criticism lies more in the direction of numerous committees in both houses and of uneven and unspecialized distribution of committee positions in the House than toward committee size. Although some Senate committees could be reduced in size, the more evident need is to abolish certain committees entirely and reorganize the remainder according to existent fields of legislation.

The second main topic, considered in an earlier chapter, is that of procedure as it relates to committees. This includes the reference of bills and the matter of meetings and hearings of the committees. What is to be desired in this field of inquiry so as to serve the assumed functions of committee systems? Specialization of knowledge and the use of expert advice, the avoidance of duplication of effort and inconsistent actions—these require consistency of reference to committees so organized as to differentiate the fields of legislation as accurately as possible. That reference of measures in all four chambers studied was often inconsistent was due partly to the fact that the existent committees do not accurately reflect the present legislative situation. Quite aside from that, however, reference was often questionable if judged by the standard mentioned above. Whatever considerations or lack of care may have caused such references, legislative efficiency demands greater accuracy and consistency than was found.

Meetings and hearings are to serve a triple function: collection of information, deliberation, and, finally, determination of the action to be recommended. In this, the committees have somewhat of a judicial nature. Collection of information requires ample opportunity for hearing those who want to contribute either facts or arguments whether they be legislators not on the committee, administrative officials, or representatives of interest-groups, public or private. Whether this necessitates a public hearing on all bills referred as is true in Massachusetts may well be debated. But the granting or refusing of a hearing should not be arbitrary, and certainly should not rest with the committee chairman alone. In general, the practice observed in Pennsylvania seemed to conform fairly well to the ideas just expressed. No case of refusal of a hearing comes to mind. Announcements of hearings seemed to be generally well in advance. While in Maryland an occasional hearing seems to have been refused, evaded, or postponed so as to be less effective, criticism lies rather in insufficient notice or lack of promptness at the time appointed. Information is collected, however, for use in final decision of the case. This requires either attendance of committee members upon hearings or such a record of proceedings as to guide the individual in his decision, or both. Both systems fall short by such measurements. Attendance is not what it should be, whether due to insufficient notice, conflicting committee demands or personal disinclination. Records of who appears and what is said are largely non-existent. These mean decreased efficiency in the legislative process which counts upon the committee system for the determination of policy.

Committee deliberation and final recommendation require also the attendance of members. This can only be secured by such assignments of members to committees as will make possible a schedule of meetings which will reduce conflicts to a minimum. With a regular schedule should go also a practice in the notification of committee members which will assure their acquaintance with time and place of meetings. Further information in the notice as to what measures are to be discussed should serve well in more careful consideration and final committee action. That the four chambers are weak when submitted to this test is repeatedly evidenced in the preceding pages.

It is particularly with respect to meetings and hearings that the joint committee system promises aid. Even if the Senate and House members of such committees should take final action separately, the system would be justified. Writing of Massachusetts, Professor A. C. HANFORD says:

. . . The joint committee system saves time and effort on the part of the members of the legislature and also that of the citizens who oppose or favor a measure; it makes possible a more careful and

10

thorough consideration of measures; gives the less experienced members of the house the benefit of the advice and suggestions from the older members of the senate; avoids shifting of responsibility and tends to reduce friction between the houses thus securing some of the advantages of a unicameral system without any of its defects.[20]

Careful study of the Maryland and Pennsylvania situations reveals the need of a committee system adjusted to accomplish these very ends. It must be said, however, both with respect to this and other proposed changes that new forms and new rules will not necessarily, and of themselves, increase the efficiency of meetings and hearings. But, at least, they will remove many obstacles to relative success that now lie in the way.

There remain those features of committee systems which serve the " agency " idea. As agents, committees supposedly expedite the business of the legislative body. Such expedition requires action by the committee within a reasonable time so that the progress of legislation may not be delayed with the attendant end-of-the-session rush. The Pennsylvania and Maryland committees, particularly in the houses of origin, are too prone to retain measures indefinitely. To be sure, the late introduction of bills, a practice more pronounced in Maryland than in Pennsylvania, contributes materially to the hurry of the closing days of the session. The committees, however, must accept a considerable share of the blame for delay. A study of the practical results of the rules providing for automatic return as found in some states would be necessary before advocating such a device. But a reorganization of the systems as indicated above involving a more even distribution of bills, combined perhaps with earlier introductions, would make greater dispatch, without the sacrifice of careful consideration, a possibility.

If, again, the committee " agent " is to recommend an action which the principal largely accepts as its own, there should be assurance that such action has been taken at a stated meeting with due notice given, that a quorum has been present, and that the recommendation was authorized by a

---

[20] A. C. Hanford, " Our Legislative Mills," in National Municipal Review, 1924, XIII, 41.

majority. The house might in its discretion require action
by a majority of the committee; in any case there should be
ready means of determining that a majority of those present
agreed. Once more, at least in certain aspects, the systems
being measured do not conform. No uniformity seems to
exist in committee practice with respect to records which
would make such a check on the agent possible. The Pennsylvania House rule requiring records apparently contributes
somewhat to the possibility of checking up the committee
action. Observation indicates, however, that due notice was
not always given and that quorums were not always present.
The Maryland records were even less satisfactory, as were the
notices of meetings and attendance of members thereat. Objections of legislators were numerous and frequent enough to
indicate that the pocketing of bills by chairmen or their
smothering by a minority was not unknown, but in recent
sessions such practices did not seem to be highly prevalent.
Where no convenient method of discharge exists, a situation
existent in Pennsylvania, the possibilities in this respect are
best understood by the legislators themselves.

Finally, the "agency" idea requires reports. If the
functions of committees be made to include the sifting of
measures, there should be a ready means of discharging a
committee from further consideration of a bill. What should
be the proper procedure may vary with circumstances, but
the requirement of anything like a majority vote seems too
difficult. If there be merit in the modern use of the referendum whereby eight or ten per cent. of the voters may bring
about a vote upon an action of the state legislature—" agent "
of the people, be it noted,—then a petition of at most one-
third of a legislative body should be sufficient to recall a
measure from a committee after a reasonable time. The
application of this measuring-stick places Maryland higher
than her sister state. Although, in practice, reports are not
required, the discharge rule, with all the restrictions upon
its use noted earlier, is still fairly effective. And its wide
endorsement, even by chairmen who had felt its effect,
indicates its worth. The Pennsylvania House rule, despite

certain endorsements, seems to the writer far too favorable to committee dominance. To secure a majority of members elected, on a measure never on the floor save for introduction, seems well-nigh impossible. Instead of serving as a means of checking the " agent," it protects instead.

Lest it be thought that the evaluation just completed is intended as derogatory of committee systems generally, the author hastens to add that such is not the case. In fact, the Maryland and Pennsylvania systems are not nearly as inefficient as they could well be under the same rules. In the interests of legislative efficiency, however, a careful reorganization of both systems would seem very advisable. The author is convinced, moreover, that no dire consequences would result from the adoption of the unicameral idea at the same time. However, further study on this point is needed.

How do the committee systems in Maryland and Pennsylvania compare with those in other states? [21] While complete studies are not numerous, comparisons can be made with those systems which have been subjected to analysis. For Illinois, Iowa, Kentucky, and Ohio, all of which have committees organized separately in each house, available studies [22] make comparisons possible.

In the matter of committee composition, all four of these studies reveal situations somewhat comparable to those enumerated above. A large number of committees or large membership, or both, resulting in multiple assignments, exist in all six states. The resultant conflicts are everywhere decried. Minority consideration of measures due to lack of attendance and the impossibility of specialization under such a system are particularly emphasized in the Ohio study. The

[21] No comparison is attempted with other studies of bicameralism. See citations at the end of ch. v.

[22] Leonard D. White, " Our Legislative Mills: The Legislative Process in Illinois," National Municipal Review, XII, 712-719; Frank E. Horack, " The Committee System," Statute Law-Making In Iowa, pp. 535-612; Kentucky Efficiency Commission, The General Assembly, Advance Pamphlet VI (1923) ; Civic League of Cleveland, Civic Affairs, No. 21 (1919). Observations upon other systems are to be found in works previously cited as well as in L. A. Frothingham, A Brief History of the Constitution and Government of Massachusetts, ch. vii (2d ed., 1925).

most extreme instance, however, is doubtless to be found in
Illinois, a situation made known by many writers. The
existence of useless or almost useless committees is also
prevalent, if measured by the distribution of bills. The
Kentucky report reads:

. . . The existence of unimportant committees gives the Speaker an
opportunity, if he is so inclined, to put members whom he desires
to punish, in places where they can do no 'harm.' From a public
point of view, all committees should be important.[23]

Horack writes:

. . . It is evident that in committees containing nearly half of the
membership of the house, the functions of investigation and deliberation must be greatly impaired.[24]

The influences that control the selection of committee members and the power of the chairman therein are discussed also
in the Illinois study.[25] In no case, save perhaps in the 1925
session of the Illinois House, do the appointments seem quite
so arbitrary as was true in the Maryland House in 1929.

In the reference of bills, the same uneven distribution and
inconsistency appear constantly. The Ohio study notes that
bills are often referred for convenience or political or personal
considerations. The practice of sending bills to different
committees in House and Senate, as noted in Maryland and
Pennsylvania, was also prevalent in Ohio. On the same
subject the Kentucky Commission remarks:

. . . Furthermore, where there are several committees covering sub-
stantially the same subjects an opportunity is given the Speaker to
play politics by referring a given bill to a committee which will give
it the sort of treatment which he desires. This makes for evasion
of responsibility.[26]

Open committee meetings with a publicly announced
schedule are demanded in Kentucky. In Iowa, despite the

[23] Op. cit., p. 14.
[24] Op. cit., p. 560.
[25] See also Cyril B. Upham, " The Speaker of the House of Representatives in Iowa " and " The President of the Senate " in Iowa
Journal of History and Politics, XVII, 68-73, 257-263; and Legislative Voters' League, Assembly Bulletin, February 7, and August
21, 1925 (Illinois).
[26] Op. cit., pp. 14-15.

customary schedule, meetings are often called to suit the convenience of the chairman.

. . . When important measures are handled in this manner, the opposition members may know nothing of the meeting until the report of the committee is made by the chairman.[27]

Complaints of pocketing led to the setting of time-limits for committee consideration in Iowa, rules, however, which are by no means always enforced.[28] None of the studies reveal so easy a means of discharge as is found in both Maryland houses. Rule 12 of the Illinois House makes the recall of bills from committee practically the same as does the difficult Pennsylvania House rule.

In general, then, it may be said that the studies covering committee systems in six states are in substantial agreement. Quite apart from the character of legislative personnel, the existent committee systems reveal a considerable degree of legislative inefficiency. Will a reorganization along the lines suggested above solve the problems discussed in this and other studies of committee systems? The answer may have to await experimentation. It is suggested, however, that a similar study in some state which has already reorganized, Nebraska for instance, might make important information available to those interested in legislation.

[27] Horack, p. 566.
[28] Ibid., p. 573; see also O. K. Patton, " Methods of Statute Law-Making in Iowa," Statute Law-Making in Iowa, pp. 223-225.

BIBLIOGRAPHY

It requires more than the reading of legislative journals, session laws, commentaries and other published matter to appreciate the role of committees in the legislative process. Acquaintance with individual legislators, committee chairmen, administrative officers, and representatives of interest-groups is quite as necessary. Attendance upon committee hearings and, if possible, upon meetings aids materially in understanding and evaluating committee systems. Newspapers are particularly valuable in giving leads concerning committee activity.

The legislative handbooks or manuals, senate and house rules, legislative journals, lists of committees, and privately published directories used in compiling the information in the first chapter are not separately listed.

ORIGINAL SOURCES

History of House Bills, Session of 1929, Harrisburg.
History of Senate Bills, Session of 1929, Harrisburg.
Journal of Proceedings of the House of Delegates of Maryland, Sessions of 1927 and 1929, Baltimore.
Journal of Proceedings of the Senate of Maryland, Sessions of 1927 and 1929, Baltimore.
Laws of the General Assembly of the Commonwealth of Pennsylvania, 1919 to 1929, Harrisburg.
Laws of the State of Maryland, 1918 to 1929, Baltimore.
Legislative Journal, 1929 (unbound), Harrisburg.
Vetoes by the Governor, Sessions of 1927 and 1929, Harrisburg.

SECONDARY SOURCES

Books:

Bates, F. G., and Field, O. P., State Government, New York, 1928.
Bryce, James, The American Commonwealth, I, 3d ed., New York, 1893.
Colvin, David Leigh, The Bicameral Principle in the New York Legislature, New York, 1913.
Cushing, Luther S., Manual of Parliamentary Practice, Albert S. Bolles, editor, Chicago, 1928.
Dodd, Walter F., and Sue H., Government in Illinois, Chicago, 1928.
Dodd, Walter F., State Government, 2d ed., New York, 1928.
Dodds, H. W., Procedure in State Legislatures, Supp. to Annals of the American Academy of Political and Social Science, lxxvii (1918).
Freund, Ernst, Standards of American Legislation, Chicago, 1917.
Frothingham, L. A., A Brief History of the Constitution and Government of Massachusetts, ch. vii, 2d ed., Boston, 1925.
Grant, James A. C., The Bicameral Principle in the California Legislature (unpublished Leland Stanford Jr. University dissertation).
Harlow, Ralph V., The History of Legislative Methods in the Period Before 1825, New Haven, 1917.
Hichborn, Franklin, Story of the Session of the California Legisla-

ture of 1909, 1911, 1913, 1915, 1917, 1919, 1921, San Francisco, 1909-1922.

Holcombe, Arthur N., State Government in the United States, 2d ed., New York, 1926.

Horack, Frank E., "The Committee System," Statute Law-Making in Iowa, Iowa City, 1916.

Ilbert, Sir Courtenay Peregrine, Legislative Methods and Forms, London, 1901.

Ilbert, Sir Courtenay Peregrine, The Mechanics of Law Making, New York, 1914.

Jones, Chester L., Statute Law Making in the United States, Boston, 1912.

Kelley, M. Clyde, Machine-Made Legislation in Pennsylvania, Pittsburgh, 1912.

Luce, Robert, Congress, An Explanation, Cambridge, 1926.

Luce, Robert, Legislative Assemblies, New York, 1924.

Luce, Robert, Legislative Principles, New York, 1930.

Luce, Robert, Legislative Procedure, New York, 1922.

McConachie, Lauros G., Congressional Committees, New York, 1898.

Mathews, John M., American State Government, New York, 1924.

Patton, O. K., "Methods of Statute Law-Making in Iowa," Statute Law-Making in Iowa, Iowa City, 1916.

Pollock, Ivan L., "Some Abuses Connected with Statute Law-Making," Statute Law-Making in Iowa, Iowa City, 1916.

Reinsch, Paul S., American Legislatures and Legislative Methods, New York, 1907.

Robert, Henry M., Parliamentary Law, New York, 1923.

Wilson, Woodrow, Congressional Government, Boston, 1890.

Magazine Articles, Pamphlets and Reports:

Bede, Elbert, "Our Legislative Mills: Oregon," National Municipal Review, XII, 536-541 (1923).

Boots, Ralph S., "Our Legislative Mills: Nebraska," National Municipal Review, XIII, 110-119 (1924).

Citizens' League, The, "Efficiency in State Legislation," Greater Cleveland, II, 175-182 (1927).

Civic League of Cleveland, "What Is Wrong with the Legislature?" Civic Affairs, No. 21 (1919).

(Illinois) Constitutional Convention Bulletins, No. 8, "The Legislative Department," Springfield, 1920.

Edson, A. W. and Hardy, R. C., "New Hampshire Legislature, 1925 Session," American Political Science Review, 19, 773-84 (1925).

Efficiency Commission, Kentucky, The General Assembly, Advance Pamphlet VI (1923).

Finty, Tom, Jr., "Our Legislative Mills: Texas," National Municipal Review, XII, 649-54 (1923).

Hall, John E., "Bicameral Principle in the New Mexico Legislature of 1925," National Municipal Review, XVI, 185-255 (1927).

Hanford, A. Chester, "Our Legislative Mills: Massachusetts," National Municipal Review, XIII, 40-48 (1924).

Hichborn, Franklin, "Suggestions for California Reorganization," American Political Science Review, VIII, 244 (1913).

Illinois Legislative Voter's League, The Assembly Bulletin (1915-1927).

Jameson, J. Franklin, "The Origin of the Standing Committee

System in American Legislative Bodies," in Political Science Quarterly, IX, 246-267 (1894).

Legislative Information Bureau, The Legislative Compendium, Chicago (1925-1929).

Massachusetts Joint Special Committee, Report, Legislative Procedure, Boston (1915).

Nebraska Legislative Reference Bureau, Bulletin No. 3, Legislative Procedure in the Forty-Eight States, Lincoln (1914).

Orth, Samuel P., "Our State Legislatures," Atlantic Monthly, December, 1904.

Schaffter, Dorothy, "The Bicameral System in Practice," Iowa Journal of History and Politics (1929).

Sheldon, Addison E., "Reform of Legislative Procedure in Nebraska," American Political Science Review, 12, 261 (1918).

Smith, C. Lysle, "The Committee System in State Legislatures," American Political Science Review, 12, 607-639 (November, 1918).

Thompson, Walter, "Our Legislative Mills: Wisconsin," National Municipal Review, XII, 600-610 (1923).

Upham, Cyril B., "The Speaker of the House of Representatives in Iowa," Iowa Journal of History and Politics, XVII, 3-82 (1918).

Upham, Cyril B., "The President of the Senate," Iowa Journal of History and Politics, XVII, 223-266 (1918).

West, Victor J., "Our Legislative Mills: California the Home of the Split Session," National Municipal Review, XII, 369-376 (1923).

White, Leonard D., "Our Legislative Mills: The Legislative Process in Illinois," National Municipal Review, XII, 712-719 (1923).

Wood-Simons, May, "Operation of the Bicameral System in Illinois and Wisconsin," Illinois Law Review, XX, 674 (1926).

INDEX

Administrative officers and legislative committees, 86, 118-121, Table 19, 119.

Amendment of recent legislation, causes, 127-128; amount, Table 21, 128; relation to committees, 127-131.

Appointment of committees, in senates, 11-13; in lower houses, 13-15; limitations upon in senates, 12-13; limitations upon in houses, 14-15; in Maryland houses, 48, 62-71; in Pennsylvania houses, 55, 62-71.

Assignments to committees, in joint systems, Table 1, 32; in bicameral systems, Table 2, 36-37; explanation and comparison, 45-47; in Maryland, Table 4, 50, Table 6, 54; relative to committee importance, Maryland, 53, Table 6, 54, 54-55; in Pennsylvania, Table 7, 56, Table 9, 60; relative to committee importance, Pennsylvania, 57, 59-61; relation to requests of members, 63; relation to occupation or profession, 63-65; relation to previous committee experience, 65-70, Table 10, 66, Table 11, 67; relation to political alignment, 70-71; to serve purposes of specialization, 143; to permit efficient committee action, 145.

Bicameral committee systems, general, 35-47; committee composition in, Table 2, 36-37.

Bicameralism, in relation to committee action, 121; in relation to governor's veto, Table 20, 121-122, 123-126; studies cited, 126 n.

Boots, Ralph S., 99 n.

Chairmen of committees, relation to occupations, 64-65; relation to committee experience, 69, 70; call committee meetings, 77, 78.

Civic League of Cleveland, 127 n, 148 n.

Colvin, David Leigh, 126 n.

Committee on rules, composition in senates, 12; acts as steering committee, 28-30; composition, 30-32; in Maryland House, 48-49; in Pennsylvania House, 55.

Committees, rules governing, general, 11-32; selection of members, 11-15; senate rules as to number and size of, 12-13; house rules as to number and size of, 14-15; reference of bills to, general, 15-17; meetings and hearings, 17-19; records, 19-21; reports, 22-26; privileged as to reports, 25-26; of conference, 26-28; steering, 28-32; composition of in joint systems, Table 1, 32; bicameral systems, general, 35-47; composition in bicameral systems, Table 2, 36-37; composition in Maryland, 48-55; work of, Maryland, 51, 53, Table 5, 52; composition in Pennsylvania, 55-57, Table 7, 56; work of, Pennsylvania, 57-59, Table 8, 58; selection of members and chairmen, 62-71; reference of measures to, 72-77; meetings, 77-84; hearings, 84-87; relation to administrative officers, 86; records of, 88-90; reports of, 90-93; discharge of, 93-99; legislative work of, 100-121; action on bills, Tables 14, 15, 16, 100-104; relation of committee action to bicameralism, 121-126; relation to early repeal or amendment of legislation, 127-131; tested by governor's veto, 131-133; tested by duplicate bills, 133-138; tested by the referendum, 138-139; functions of, 139-141; desiderata in order to perform accepted functions, 142-148; comparisons of systems in several states, 148-150.

155